JEFF MacNELLY

AVON
PUBLISHERS OF BARD, CAMELOT AND DISCUS BOOKS

SHOE is an original publication of Avon Books. This work has never before appeared in book form.

AVON BOOKS
A division of
The Hearst Corporation
959 Eighth Avenue
New York, New York 10019
Library of Congress Catalog Card Number: 78-57643

Published by arrangement with the author.
Library of Congress Catalog Card Number:
ISBN: 0-380-40154-1

First Avon Printing, November, 1978

Printed in the U.S.A.

8275 Avon Books (Jeff McNelly) 5 4 3 2 1 (Alphatype) 6-5-78
9 Windsor Light 3 Repros

For Rita

MacNelly As Seen by Another Artist,

Jeff MacNelly has many things in common with the great artists of the Western world—with these exceptions: He is three and a half times taller than Toulouse-Lautrec, has twice as much hair as Pablo Picasso, and although he has suffered more than Vincent van Gogh, he still has both his ears.

Mr. MacNelly founded the Virginia Neo-Realist school of bird painting. He turned his back on Audubon, Whistler, and Walt Disney, and decided to add new dimensions to feathered creatures—dimensions which no artist had ever dared paint before. One, for example, was to put sneakers on P. Martin Shoemaker's feet. Another was to insert a cigar in his mouth. A third was to have him sit at the typewriter, and a fourth was to show him using a telephone.

Almost every art critic in the world laughed when they saw MacNelly's early work. But they aren't laughing anymore. As Timothy Cruecook wrote in Art Be Damned, "Who are we to say that birds don't talk to each other, or do not have their own newspapers, or that their best friends aren't called, 'Perfesser'?" MacNelly, with one stroke of his brush, has seared our conscience, and has grabbed us by the throat and made us sit up in our chairs, and admit it is we, not he, who are marching to a different drummer.

In this book, which is a retrospective of MacNelly's "bird period," we see the tormented soul of MacNelly, who at twenty-nine years old rejected the commercialism of Rothko, Rauschenberg, and Wyeth, and went out on a limb. His ecstatically moving forms open up on familiar scenes, yet unlike Tintoretto, they are warm rather than severe. But there is more here than the eye perceives.

To understand it, you must understand the man behind Shoe.

Jeff MacNelly is what is known in the art world as a "double dipper." In the daytime he draws a political cartoon, which appears in three-hundred newspapers. At night, he locks himself in a garret to turn out this comic strip. He does it because he needs the money. Saddled with a wife and two children, MacNelly barely ekes out a living from his two jobs. But, as so many artists before him, he would rather starve than sell out for commercial reasons.

Art Buchwald

That is why MacNelly went into birds. "Birds," he told me when he started this strip, "are not commercial, unless they talk."

"But your birds talk," I told him.

"Yes," he said, "but not for money."

One cannot underestimate the influence of having to live in Richmond, Virginia on MacNelly's work. Although he originally came from Cedarhurst, Long Island, his years in the South have taken their toll on him. As you will see as you turn the pages, MacNelly puts his characters up a tree and leaves them there.

He even puts roller skates on one of his birds because he cannot fly. No sane person, who lived in the North, would attempt to get away with this nonsense.

And yet, perhaps he is saying something to all of us...something like "The country is for the birds," or "There is more to life than Jonathan Seagull."

Whatever his message is, I think we should listen, because Shoe, like Michelangelo's painting on the ceiling of the Sistine Chapel, has something to tell us about ourselves. It reminds us that no man is an island and, if we don't stop to smell the flowers, we will never hear the voice of the turtle.

If that last paragraph doesn't make any sense to you, it's about time you turned the page and got on with the book.

Then go out and buy the sweat shirt. By Christmas, there should be enough Shoe dolls in the stores to satisfy everybody. In a few years you may take your children to "MacNellyland," which is now on the drawing boards.

But never throw this book away. Someday it will be a collector's item, worth three Doonesburys or six Peanuts. Mine has already been placed in a safe deposit box at the Riggs National Bank. It is the only thing I have of value to leave to my children.

March, 1978

Foreword

When we first asked Jeff MacNelly to develop a comic strip for us, his laconic reply was, "I've got enough to do." And so he did—a daily editorial cartoon, spot art for his newspaper, illustrations for a syndicated feature, splendid watercolors. In the cartooning business, his regimen was more than a full plate. It was a groaning board.

It is a commonplace observation in the arts, however, that the most talented people are the most productive people, and the easiest to work with. And so it proved to be with Jeff. He took to Shoe like, well, a bird to flight. As fuzzy notions were translated into stunning reality by his drawings, we found ourselves saying repeatedly, "That's it exactly!" The family of characters grew and prospered—P. Martin Shoemaker, the Perfesser, Loon, Roz, Irving Seagull, and the rest.

Shoe made its debut on September 12, 1977. Since then it has spread around the world, appearing now in 440 newspapers. In this short span of life, it has become the most popular new comic strip in years. Its sly sophistication and anthropomorphic magic seem to appeal to readers of all ages, in all circumstances. I suspect that, 122 pages hence, you will understand why. Happy landings!

April, 1978
Vienna, Virginia

Neal B. Freeman
Jefferson Communications, Inc.

FOR YOUR CONVENIENCE, I'VE DIVIDED THIS BOOK INTO THREE PARTS: ONE, TWO AND C.

RRING!
TRASH

HELLO. THIS IS P. MARTIN SHOEMAKER SPEAKING...
MACNELLY

WHILE I AM OUT OF THE OFFICE MY CALLS ARE BEING HANDLED BY AN AUTOMATIC ANSWERING DEVICE. IF YOU WANT TO LEAVE A MESSAGE, START SPEAKING AT THE SOUND OF THE **CLICK.**

CLICK.

ANOTHER LETTER TO THE EDITOR, SHOE?...
YEAH. AND THIS TIME THAT CLOWN BETTER PRINT IT.
9/13
WELL... WHADDYA THINK?
I THINK YOU MIGHT WANT TO END IT A LITTLE MORE CORDIALLY.
MACNELLY
WHY? WHAT'S WRONG WITH "STICK IT IN YER KAZOO"?

Dear Editor:
In my last letter to you I told you to "stick it in your kazoo." I apologize for that remark.
9/14
MACNELLY

It was uncalled for, snide, and totally disrespectful to you and your fine newspaper. Please allow me to rewrite that ill-conceived letter:

Dear Editor:
While wrapping some catfish the other night, I noticed an item on your editorial page.

WHY DON'T THEY EVER PRINT YOUR LETTERS TO THE EDITOR?

I DON'T KNOW, PERFESSER...
MACNELLY

MAYBE I'M JUST TOO SUBTLE FOR 'EM.
9/15

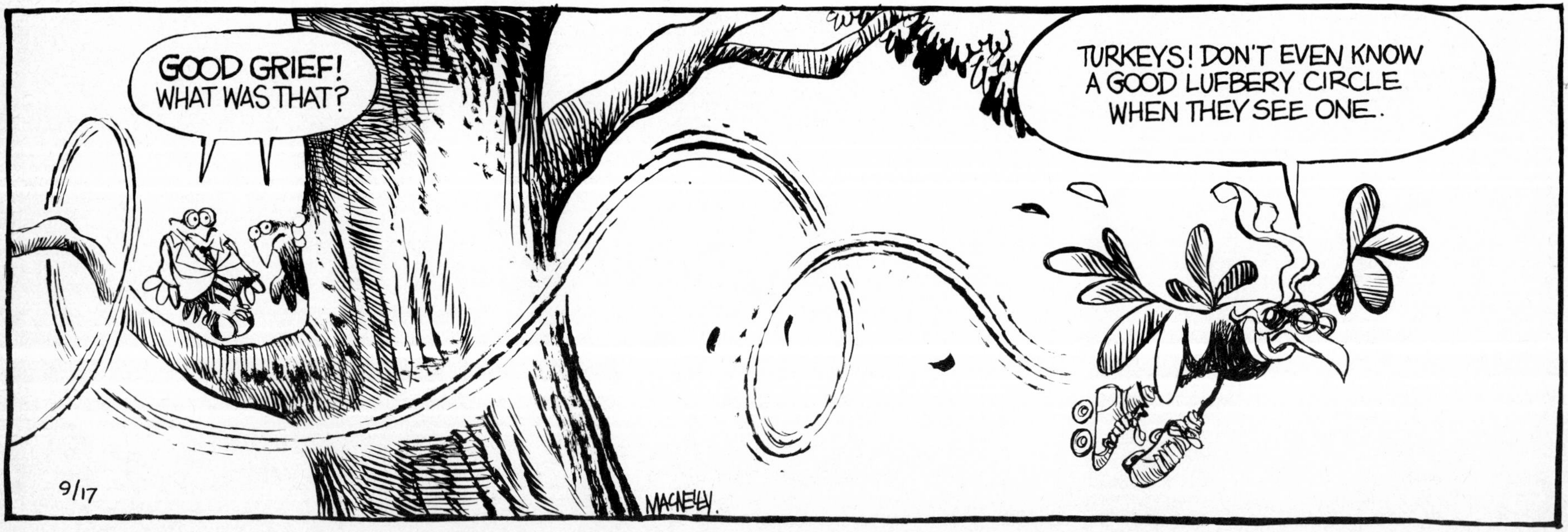

GOOD GRIEF! WHAT WAS THAT?

TURKEYS! DON'T EVEN KNOW A GOOD LUFBERY CIRCLE WHEN THEY SEE ONE.

9/17

MACNELLY.

2.0
1.5
1.5
MACNELLY
9/19

NOW, LOON, BEFORE YOU TAKE OFF, BE SURE TO CHECK THE WINDSOCK.
WINDSOCK?

YEAH... IT'S A SOCK THAT TELLS YOU THE WIND DIRECTION. YOU SHOULD ALWAYS CHECK IT OUT BEFORE TAKE-OFF.

SNIFF... NORTH-NORTHEAST I'D SAY.
MACNELLY 9/20

WELL, THIS IS IT...
MY FIRST SOLO.

GEE, I'M SCARED! WHAT IF I GET AIRSICK?...OR OVERSHOOT THE RUNWAY?

...OR GET LOST?
MACNELLY 9/21

...OR RUN OUT OF QUARTERS?
25¢

NOW REMEMBER, MY BOY, IF YOU GET IN TROUBLE...
PULL THE RIPCORD.

BUT ONLY IF YOU'RE SURE YOU CAN'T MAKE IT.
9 22

GERONIMO.
MACNELLY

9
23
MACNELLY

THERE GOES THE FIRST STUDENT PILOT IN AVIATION HISTORY WHO OUGHTA BE GETTIN' COMBAT PAY.

I THINK LOON'S GOT A GREAT FUTURE.
DOING WHAT?

SKYWRITIN'

IN ARABIC.
MACNELLY
9
24

OKAY, PERFESSER, THE OBJECT IN BACKPACKING IS TO TRAVEL AS LIGHTLY AS POSSIBLE. SO... PACK JUST THE BARE ESSENTIALS.

RIGHT, SHOE... JUST THE ESSENTIALS. LET'S SEE IF I'VE GOT EVERYTHING.
MACNELLY

...ELECTRIC BLANKET... GALOSHES, A CASE OF BREW, MICROWAVE OVEN, T.V., BOWLING BALL...
JOISEY CITY
9/26

YOU MEAN I GOTTA SCHLEP THIS SUITCASE AROUND ALL DAY, AND SLEEP OUTSIDE ALL NIGHT? THIS BACKPACKING STUFF IS **ABSURD**!

—NOT ONLY THAT... IT'S **SUBVERSIVE**! IT UNDERMINES A GREAT AMERICAN **TRADITION**...

COMFORT.
MACNELLY
9/27

AW, COME ON, PERFESSER... YOU'LL LOVE IT OUT HERE IN THE GREAT OUTDOORS —CLOSE TO NATURE...

I DON'T MIND THE GREAT OUTDOORS, BUT LET'S NOT GET TOO CLOSE TO NATURE... OKAY?
9/28
MACNELLY

THIS IS A GREAT SPOT, EH, PERFESSER? LOOK AT THAT VIEW!

LET'S MAKE CAMP RIGHT OVER HERE...
9/29
MACNELLY

COULDN'T WE FIND A SPOT CLOSER TO THE MEN'S ROOM?

OKAY, PERFESSER...
LET'S PITCH THE TENT.
MACNELLY

GOOD!...DARNED THING
WAS TOO HEAVY ANYWAY.
9/30

OKAY, WHAT'LL IT BE?
...WE GOT FRANKS AN' BEANS, PEACHES, PEAS...
NO, THANKS, SHOE. I'VE MADE MY OWN DINNER PLANS... WHERE'S A PHONE?

WE'RE NOWHERE NEAR A PHONE...
OH?

ROZ! A LARGE PEPPERONI TO GO! DOUBLE CHEESE!
10/1
MACNELLY

READY THE NUMBER ONE CATAPULT!
10/3

STAND BY TO LAUNCH AIRCRAFT!

WHOOSH
MACNELLY

I WONDER IF JIMMY DOOLITTLE STARTED OUT THIS WAY...

WAY TO GO, LOON! AN AVIATION FIRST!
MACNELLY

A PERFECT ONE POINT LANDING.
10/4

LOON, YOUR CATAPULT SYSTEM SEEMS TO WORK... WHAT ABOUT YOUR BRAKES?
PUT IT THIS WAY, PERFESSER...

I CAN STOP ON A DIME....
MACNELLY 10/5

THIS TIME I'VE GOT TO PULL UP FAST...

TO MISS THIS TR...

BONK!
MACNELLY 10/6

WHAT'S THAT
UP AHEAD?...OH NO!
WHAT EVERY PILOT
DREADS!

CAW!
CAW
CAW
CAW!

STARLING
IN THE
INTAKE!
MACNELLY 10/7

LOON, I THINK THAT
WE COULD KEEP YOU
ALOFT IF WE APPLY
SOME OF THE PRINCIPLES
OF THE NOBLE **BLIMP**
TO YOUR FLYING
PROBLEM.
MACNELLY 10/8

IF ONLY
THERE WERE
A WAY TO
FILL YOU
WITH **GAS**.

ROZ'S
ROOST
ROZ!
ONE LARGE
PIZZA TO GO
—DOUBLE
PEPPERONI.

GEE, ROZ... IS THIS ALL YOU'RE SERVIN' TODAY— THIS GRUBBY HEALTH FOOD?
OH, SHUT UP AND TRY IT, SHOE... IT'S GOOD FOR YOU.
MACNELLY

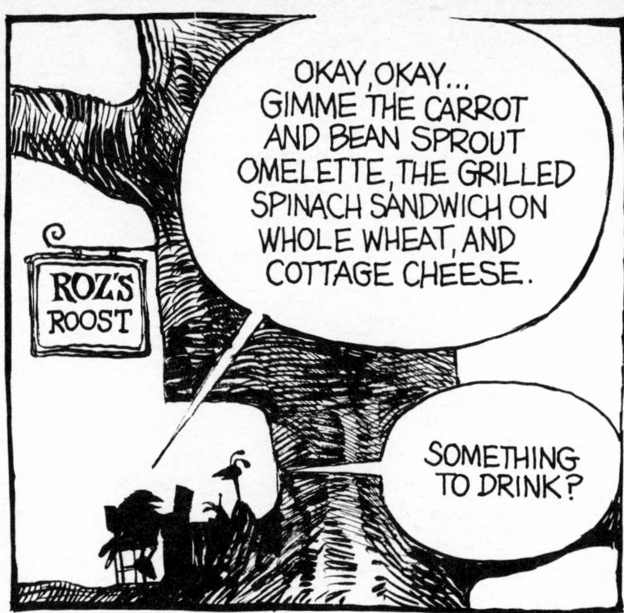
ROZ'S ROOST
OKAY, OKAY... GIMME THE CARROT AND BEAN SPROUT OMELETTE, THE GRILLED SPINACH SANDWICH ON WHOLE WHEAT, AND COTTAGE CHEESE.
SOMETHING TO DRINK?

A ROOT BEER FLOAT.
MENU
10/10

YOU GOTTA DO SOMETHING ABOUT THIS COFFEE, ROZ... YUKKY!

WHAT'S WRONG WITH MY COFFEE, YOU LITTLE LIZARD?
HOLD IT, ROZ! —I'M NOT THE ONLY ONE. THE PERFESSER DOESN'T LIKE IT MUCH, EITHER, DO YOU, PERFESSER?
MACNELLY
10/11
WHAT?

MY UNEMPLOYMENT PREDICAMENT HAS REALLY GOT ME DOWN, ROZ.
ROZ'S ROOST
COME ON, PERFESSER, YOU'RE A SMART GUY... YOU'LL FIND SOMETHING...

HOW LONG HAVE YOU BEEN LOOKING?
SINCE JUNE.

MACNELLY 10/12
OF 1938.

OUT OF WORK SINCE 1938?... GEE, PERFESSER, THAT'S A LONG TIME. —BUT I THOUGHT YOU HAD A FANCY DEGREE IN SOMETHING.
SPECIAL:

YES, ROZ... I WAS PHI BETA KAPPA AT RUTGERS, AND GOT A PH.D. IN AERODYNAMIC DESIGN.
WOW.

BUT I MAJORED IN BLIMPS.
MACNELLY 10/13

ROZ'S ROOST
THERE MUST BE SOME JOB FOR A GUY WITH YOUR UNIQUE TALENT AND ABILITY, PERFESSER.
I'M AFRAID NOT, ROZ.
MACNELLY 10/14

IT'S QUITE A SPECIALIZED FIELD, YOU KNOW...

I'LL SAY IT IS. WHEN WAS THE LAST TIME YOU SAW AN AD THAT SAID, "WANTED: BLIMP DESIGNER"?

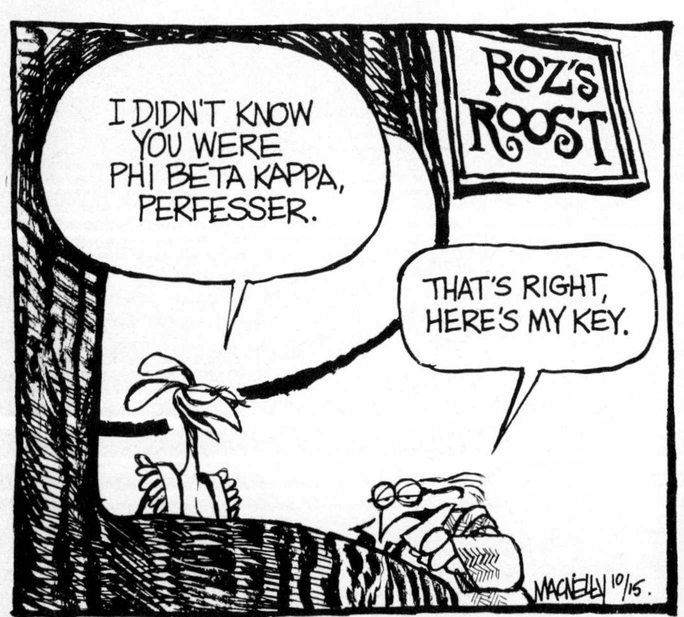
ROZ'S ROOST
I DIDN'T KNOW YOU WERE PHI BETA KAPPA, PERFESSER.
THAT'S RIGHT, HERE'S MY KEY.
MACNELLY 10/15.

OH YEAH... GEE, THAT'S NICE....DOES IT UNLOCK ANYTHING?
NO...NOT REALLY...

BUT I DID USE IT TO JIMMY OPEN A COKE MACHINE ONCE

I ALMOST FORGOT! TODAY'S MONDAY...

THE GARBAGEMAN COMES TODAY...
MACNELLY
10/17

TO GIVE ME AN ESTIMATE.

ONE OF THESE DAYS I'VE GOT TO GET ON THE STICK AND GET THIS PIG PEN ORGANIZED!

THERE MUST BE SOME KIND OF EASY SYSTEM...
SO THAT EVERYTHING IS FILED UNDER ITS OWN... HMM...
MACNELLY

MISCELLANEOUS
10/18

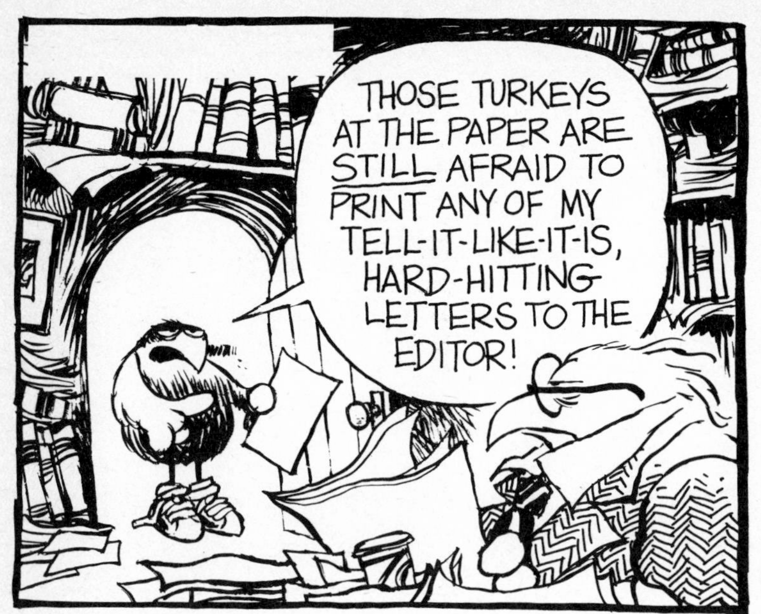
THOSE TURKEYS AT THE PAPER ARE STILL AFRAID TO PRINT ANY OF MY TELL-IT-LIKE-IT-IS, HARD-HITTING LETTERS TO THE EDITOR!

HERE'S THE LATEST REJECT....NOW, TELL ME, PERFESSER, WHAT COULD POSSIBLY BE WRONG WITH THAT, HUH?
HMMM... SEEMS TO BE WELL WRITTEN, WELL THOUGHT OUT, ... LOGICALLY PUT TOGETHER.... ER, BUT, SHOE...
DO YOU REALLY THINK WE NEED A "NATIONAL KICK-A-CAT DAY?"
MACNELLY 10/19

BAH! THE ONLY WAY I'LL EVER GET ANYTHING PUBLISHED IS TO START MY OWN NEWSPAPER.
NOT A BAD IDEA...

THEN YOU COULD WRITE LETTERS-TO-THE-EDITOR TO YOURSELF.
MACNELLY 10/20

THERE. I'VE GOT A DESK, A TELEPHONE, A TYPEWRITER...

WHAT ELSE DO I NEED TO START A NEWSPAPER?
10/21
MACNELLY

THE BEST LIBEL LAWYER ON THE EAST COAST.

HEY, I NEED A NAME FOR THIS NEWSPAPER I'M STARTING, PERFESSER.
EDITOR

THINK OF SOMETHING THAT SAYS "NEWSPAPER"... —A NAME THAT SYMBOLIZES THE SPIRIT OF MODERN JOURNALISM...

Tribune
The TREETOPS TATTLER!
10/22
MACNELLY

RING!

HELLO?...
10/24

NO. THIS IS NOT DIAL-A-JOKE! THIS IS P. MARTIN SHOEMAKER.

YOU'LL DO.
MACNELLY
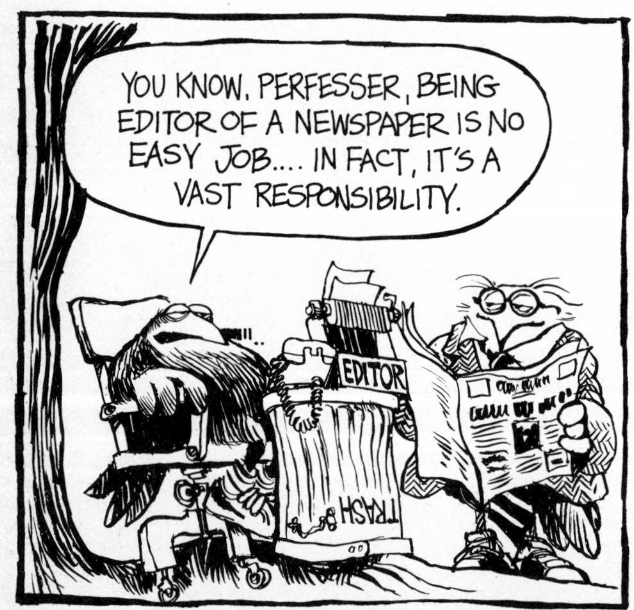
YOU KNOW, PERFESSER, BEING EDITOR OF A NEWSPAPER IS NO EASY JOB.... IN FACT, IT'S A VAST RESPONSIBILITY.
EDITOR
TRASH

THE NEWSPAPER IS MANY THINGS: RIGHTER OF WRONGS, DEFENDER OF FREEDOM...SEEKER OF TRUTH, DISPENSER OF WISDOM...
MACNELLY 10/25

WRAPPER OF FISH, AND KEEPER OF THE BASEBALL STANDINGS.
EDITOR

SAY, PERFESSER... I COULD REALLY USE A GOOD REPORTER ON THE TATTLER-TRIBUNE... YOU GOT ANY EXPERIENCE?
NOT REALLY, SHOE. I HAD A SHORT STINT AS THE SUNDAY EDITOR...
EDITO
MACNELLY 10/26.

SUNDAY EDITOR?! ARE YOU KIDDIN'? THAT'S A BIG JOB...

...FOR THE SATURDAY EVENING POST.

THERE'S ONLY ONE REAL PROBLEM WITH JOURNALISM...
TAP TAP TAP
XXX

TAP TAP
XXX
MACNELLY
10/27

EDITORS.
TAP
TAP TAP TAP

NOW WHERE THE HECK IS THAT PEN?

GEEZ...I WAS JUST USING IT.

IT COULDN'T HAVE JUST DISAPPEARED!
MACNELLY 10/28

I DON'T KNOW, MAYBE I PUT IT BACK IN MY...

POCKET.

TATTLER Tribune

I WISH THAT PAPERBOY WOULD HIT THE FRONT STEP ONCE IN A WHILE.
YER LUCKY I HIT THE TREE AT ALL, PAL.
MACNELLY 10/29

WHAT'S THIS?... A LETTER FROM MY NEPHEW, SKYLER.
PROF. COSMO FISHHAWK

IT'S EITHER BAD NEWS OR MONEY...
NO... I'M WRONG...
MACNELLY 10/31

IT'S BOTH. HE'S COMING TO STAY FOR A WHILE, AND HE NEEDS 20 BUCKS TO GET HERE.

HEY, UNCLE COSMO!
HI THERE, SKYLER. HOW WAS THE TRIP?

OH... YOU KNOW HOW IT GOES ON A BUS TRIP, UNCLE COZ. I WAS SEATED IN SAFE, SPEEDY, CONVENIENT, AIR-CONDITIONED COMFORT...

NEXT TO A 400-POUND WINO WITH CHIGGERS.
MACNELLY 11/1

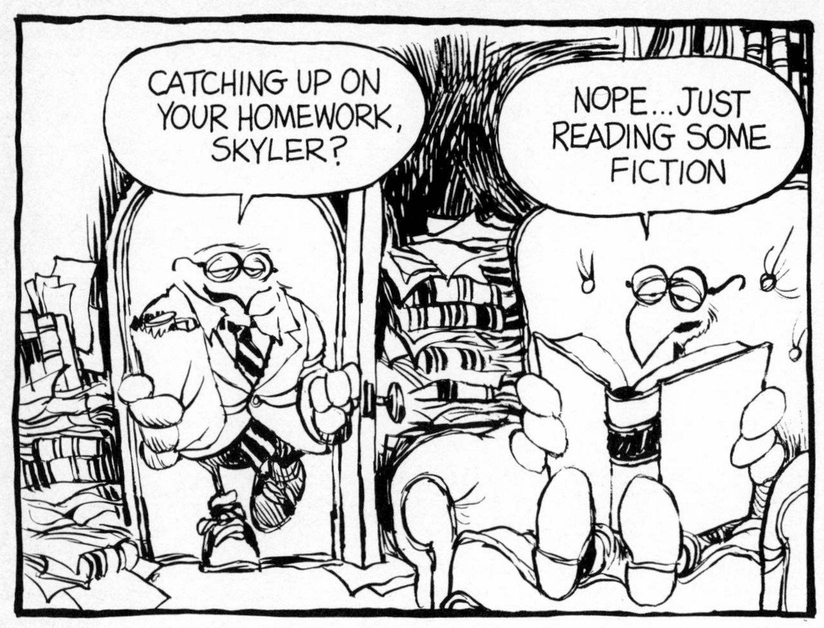

HOLD IT, SKY... CALM DOWN! THERE ARE BETTER WAYS TO DEAL WITH BULLIES LIKE HIM. JUST REMEMBER... HE PROBABLY HAS PROBLEMS, SO TRY TO TALK TO HIM — ACT FRIENDLY, BE UNDERSTANDING, TRY TO GAIN HIS CONFIDENCE...

WHAT ARE YOU UP TO NOW, SKYLER?
I'M STUDYING **KARATE**....WATCH THIS, UNCLE COZ...
AAH
EEE!
FOOM!
11/4

PHONE

FOR GOOD TIME CALL KL5-1276
PHONE

PHONE

PHONE
DIAL DIAL
MACNELLY
11/7

AT THE TONE THE TIME WILL BE... 2:20

MACNELLY 8/11
WELL, LOON... WHO ARE YOU VOTING FOR TODAY?
I DON'T KNOW, PERFESSER...
I WAS JUST ABOUT TO FLIP THIS QUARTER TO SEE.

OH, GOOD!.. HEADS!
GEORGE WASHINGTON.

HERE COMES THE COMIC SECTION...

PERFESSER, I'D LIKE TO REGISTER FOR YOUR SERIES OF LECTURES
CERTAINLY ... DID YOU BRING THE TUITION?

HAVE A SEAT, MY DEAR.

TODAY'S LECTURE TOPIC IS "EXTINCTION: ITS CAUSES AND PREVENTION."

AS YOU NO DOUBT REALIZE, THERE ARE MANY VARIETIES OF EXTINCT SPECIES...

BUT TODAY WE SHALL FOCUS ON ONE CRITTER FROM WITHIN OUR OWN FEATHERED FAMILY, THE DIDUS INEPTUS.....KNOWN OTHERWISE AS DODO.
DODO

"A CURIOUS-LOOKING, CLUMSY-FOOTED CREATURE, TOTALLY INCAPABLE OF FLYING,

THE DODO HAS BEEN EXTINCT FOR 300 YE....

GET ME THE MUSEUM OF NATURAL HISTORY.
MACNELLY 9/18

COMING IN
FOR A
LANDING...

...ON FINAL
APPROACH.

GEAR
DOWN!

FLAPS DOWN!

THROTTLE BACK... STEADY...STEADY! NOSE UP, NOW... EASY DOES IT... TOUCHDOWN!

OKAY... HIT THE BRAKES.

HARDER...

MORE BRAKES!
KRONCH

BUSH LEAGUE AIRPORT! I WOULDA HAD PLENTY OF RUNWAY IN DALLAS.
MACNELLY 9-25

YOU'LL LOVE BACKPACKING... ONCE YOU'VE BEEN BITTEN BY THE BUG.

BITTEN ONCE, I WOULDN'T MIND... ...

THIS IS IT, MAN!... THE CALL OF THE WILD, THE CHALLENGE OF THE GREAT OUTDOORS!

I DON'T MIND WALKING AROUND IN THE GREAT OUTDOORS...

BUT DO WE HAVE TO SLEEP IN IT?

THAT'S WHAT IT'S ALL ABOUT, PERFESSER... EACH OF US OUT HERE, ONE ON ONE WITH MOTHER NATURE... A TEST OF SURVIVAL IN A HOSTILE ENVIRONMENT
THAT REMINDS ME, I FORGOT TO PACK MY TOASTER.

HEY, I THINK WE'RE GETTING NEAR THE NATIONAL PARK...
REALLY? HOW DO YOU KNOW?
MACNELLY

OH, I CAN JUST TELL.
10-2

AIRBORNE AT LAST!...OKAY, JETTISON BOOSTER ROCKET!

OH, NO!

TWANGA
TWING
TWING
TWANG

TWANGA
TWING!

TWUNG
TWONG
TINK
DINK
DINGA
TONK

ZANG
ZONK
ZINGA
ZINK
ZANG

ROZ'S ROOST
INKA
PLUNK
PLINK
DINK
BINKA
DINK

HELLO?... "GUINNESS BOOK OF WORLD RECORDS"? ...I GOT A GUY HERE WHO JUST PLAYED "DUELING BANJOS" ON A SET OF HIGH VOLTAGE WIRES
MACNELLY 10/9

EASY, NOW!

CAREFUL, SHOE!
UMPH!

HOLD IT, SHOE... LET'S SET IT DOWN RIGHT HERE.
OOF!

WHADDYA WANT WITH A PIANO ANYWAY, HUH, PERFESSER?

YOU DON'T HAVE ANY ROOM FOR IT IN THIS MESS.

THERE. ISN'T THAT GREAT? I'VE ALWAYS WANTED ONE OF THESE!
WHAT FOR? YOU DON'T EVEN PLAY THE PIANO...
MACNELLY 10/16

I KNOW, BUT IT MAKES A DYNAMITE PAPERWEIGHT.

HAVING TROUBLE WITH THE PHONE?
YEAH, IRV.

IT RINGS TOO MUCH.

WHILE I'M HERE I COULD INSTALL A HOLD BUTTON ON YOUR PHONE.

IT MIGHT COME IN HANDY.
THANKS ANYWAY, IRV...

BUT I DON'T NEED A HOLD BUTTON.

I USE THIS EXTRA LONG PHONE CORD.

INSTEAD OF HOLD?
THAT'S RIGHT...
RING!

WATCH.
RRING!

HELLO... TREETOPS TATTLER-TRIBUNE -COULD YOU HOLD, PLEASE?

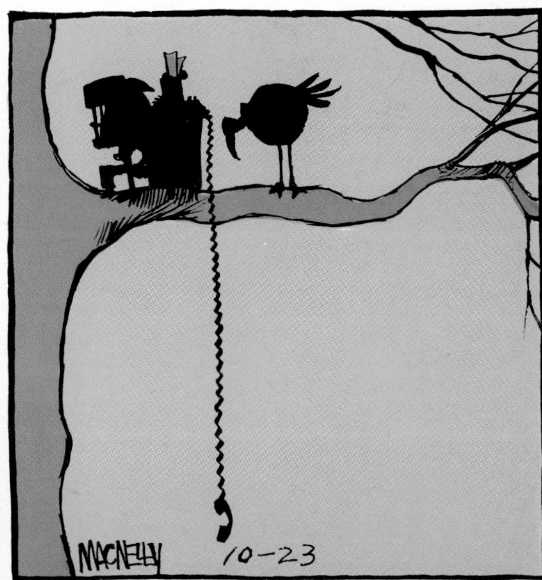
MACNELLY
10-23

NOW WHERE DID I PUT MY SNEAKERS?
TUNA

WELL, HERE'S THE LEFT ONE...
LEFT
etc.

AND THE RIGHT....
OTHER

PERFESSER
AH! WHAT A GREAT DAY FOR A WORKOUT!

UMPH

OOF

OOMF!

PERFESSER
GRUMPH! PANT PANT

WHEEZ

THERE! PHEW!

THAT'S ALL FOR TODAY...
DON'T WANT TO STRAIN ANYTHING THE FIRST TIME OUT.
MACNELLY 10/30

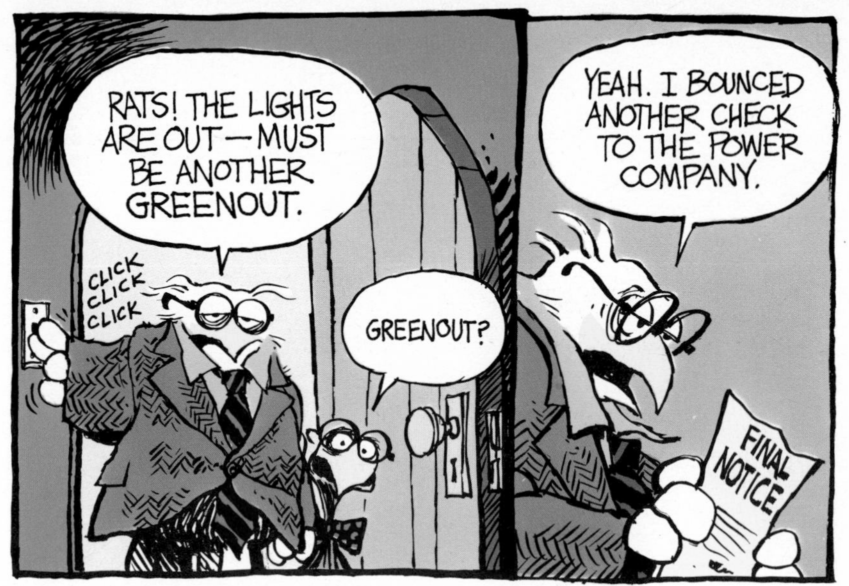
RATS! THE LIGHTS ARE OUT—MUST BE ANOTHER GREENOUT.
CLICK CLICK CLICK
GREENOUT?
YEAH. I BOUNCED ANOTHER CHECK TO THE POWER COMPANY.
FINAL NOTICE

IT'S REALLY GETTING CHILLY IN HERE WITH THE POWER OFF, SKYLER...
SURE IS, UNCLE COSMO... MAYBE WE SHOULD LIGHT A FIRE

THAT WOULD BE NICE, BUT I'M NOT VERY GOOD AT BUILDING FIRES.

BUT I MAY HAVE SOMETHING IN MY LIBRARY THAT MIGHT BE USEFUL...

COL. FRIED
AH, YES... HERE IT IS.

A HANDBOOK ON WILDERNESS SURVIVAL... SEE IF THAT WILL HELP YOU BUILD A FIRE.
MACNELLY 11/6

YEP... THAT'S GOT IT STARTED, NOW HAND ME A COUPLE OF VOLUMES OF THE ENCYCLOPEDIA...

ROZ'S ROOST
HEY, ROZ! GIMME A NUMBER 4, WILL YA?

YOU WANNA HOLD THE SPINACH, RIGHT?
RIGHT.
BLAT!

I'LL HAVE A PIECE OF THAT BOSTON CREAM PIE, PLEASE, ROZ...
NO.

ROZ'S ROOST
NO?! WHADDYA MEAN, NO?
NO PIE FOR YOU, PAL...

NOW LOOK, ROZ! I'M A PAYIN' CUSTOMER! I ORDERED PIE! I WANT SOME PIE!
NOPE.

AW, COME ON, ROZ... PLEASE?
YOU KNOW THE RULES.

ROZ'S ROOST

ONLY DINER IN THE WORLD WHERE THEY MAKE YOU EAT ALL YOUR GREEN BEANS.

I DON'T BELIEVE IT!

SHERMAN "SHOTGUN" SCHUBERT JUST DISLOCATED HIS ELBOW...

DOIN' A BEER COMMERCIAL.

OH NO! THE TURKEYS HAVE THE BALL... FIRST AND GOAL ON THE TWO!
AND THEY CAN'T MOVE!

SO THEY TRY A FIELD GOAL AND BLOW IT!

YOU'D THINK THAT A TEAM THAT CAN'T RUN, CAN'T PASS, AND CAN'T CATCH WOULD AT LEAST BE ABLE TO PUNT ONCE IN A WHILE! BUT NOT THESE CLOWNS!

THEY CAN'T EVEN KICK OFF STRAIGHT!

YOU CAN'T PLAY THE GAME IF YOU CAN'T EVEN KICK THE BALL!

CRAK

MACNELLY 11/20

HIRE THE GUY WHO PUNTED THAT TV SET!
T
Turkeys

T-T.

HERE IT IS, GANG!
MACNELLY 11/27

THE FIRST SUNDAY EDITION OF THE TREETOPS TATTLER-Tribune!
TREETOPS TATTLER-Tribune

ROZ's ROOST
HEY, THAT'S **GREAT,** SHOE!
WOW!
CONGRATS!

LET ME SEE THE SPORTS SECTION...
SURE.

ROOST
RIP RIP

WELL... IT **IS** JUST OUR FIRST SUNDAY EDITION...
TREETOPS TATTLER-Tribune
SPORTS

Bagpipes

I TAKE A LOT OF GRIEF AROUND HERE ABOUT MY BAGPIPES
MACNELLY
12/4

BUT I'LL WIN OVER A BUNCH OF CONVERTS...

WITH MY HAUNTINGLY IRRESISTIBLE RENDITION OF "THE BLUEBELLS OF SCOTLAND."

SKAREE

KRREEE
SCORAWK
A-RONK!

Newsroom
TRASH

TICKA
TICK...SPROING
EDITO

THAT DOES IT, SHOE! I NEED A NEW TYPEWRITER. THIS THING HAS REALLY BITTEN THE DUST...
NEVER.
THAT'S A PERFECTLY GOOD MACHINE--IT MADE IT THROUGH A WHOLE WAR...
YEAH. THE @★?!! CRIMEAN WAR. LOOK... I GOT THE E KEY HERE IN MY HAND...

IT KINDA LIMITS MY SUBJECT MATTER IF I CAN'T TYPE E...

Newsroo
DON'T YOU THINK THE NEWSPAPER COULD SPRING FOR A NEW TYPEWRITER?
TRASH

LOOK, PERFESSER, I GOT A LOT TO DO... YOU GOT A COMPLAINT?... WRITE ME A MEMO!
OKAY.

Mmo.
To: P. Martin Shomakr.
From: Profssor Cosmo Fishawk.
Dar Sho:
You ar a CHAPSKAT!
12/11
MACNELLY

HOW'S THE JUNK HARVEST COMING, IRV?

YOU WANNA SEE A REAL BUMPER CROP?
41UA

QUITE AN OPERATION YOU GOT HERE, IRV.... WHERE DID YOU GET ALL THIS STUFF?
JUNKING IS JUST LIKE FARMING, PERFESSER.

YOU HAVE TO GROW YOUR JUNK, Y'KNOW?...PLANT IT, CULTIVATE IT...
IRVING SEAGULL JUNKSTER
MACNELLY 12/18

AND YOU HAVE SEASONS IN JUNKING, JUST LIKE IN FARMING.

BUT THIS IS MY FAVORITE SEASON.
YOU'RE RIGHT, IRV. THIS IS A HAPPY SEASON... SANTA CLAUS, CHRISTMAS CAROLS, THE KIDS AND THEIR **TOYS**...

IRVING'S
THOSE AREN'T TOYS, PERFESSER...

THEY'RE **JUNK** SEEDLINGS.

HEY, SHOE...
YOU BELIEVE
IN SANTA CLAUS?

OF COURSE NOT.
GET SERIOUS...
GEEZ!

SHOEMAKER,
...P. MARTIN...
ONE TINY LUMP
OF COAL.

BOY, UNCLE COSMO...
SANTA CLAUS SURE
HAS A ROUGH JOB!

ALL THOSE KIDS
TO KEEP TRACK OF!
ALL THE
LETTERS
TO READ!

ALL THE TOYS HE HAS TO BUILD!

ALL THAT TRAVELING IN ONE NIGHT!

MACNELLY 12/25
...NOT TO MENTION ALL THE ✱!! ENVIRONMENTAL IMPACT STATEMENTS I GOTTA FILE FOR THESE FLYING REINDEER!
Merry Christmas

HEY, GREAT! THE RIVER'S FROZEN.

STAND BY FOR A DEMONSTRATION OF THE FINE ART OF FIGURE SKATING!

OOPS.

WHOOOMP

MACNELLY 1/1
I SEE HE'S STARTING WITH THE BASIC FIGURE ONE.

ARF ARF

LET'S SEE... WHO SHOULD I SOCK IT TO TODAY?...

YIKES! IT'S THAT HUNTER AND HIS DUMB DOG AGAIN!
BLAM
BLAM!
ARF! ARF!

THIS CALLS FOR ONE OF MY SEARING ANTI-HUNTING EDITORIALS.

TAKKA-TAKKA-TAKKADA-TAP-TAP-TAP-TAP-TADDAP-TAPPA-
DING!

ZZING!
ARF! ARF!

TAKKADA-TAP-TAP-TAP-TADDAPPA-TAP--DING!

ZING!

TAPPATAPPA TAPPATAPPA DING!
BLAM! BLAM!
GO GIT IT, BOY!!....

ZING!
MACNELLY 1/8

NOW THIS IS GONNA BE TOUGH TO EXPLAIN!

ANY SCORE YET?
YEAH...

BEER 3 — SHAVING CREAM 2.

WE'LL BE BACK WITH THE STARTING LINEUPS... AFTER THIS IMPORTANT MESSAGE:
TAKE TIME OUT FOR THE ICE-COLD, TINGLING FLAVOR OF Belch Bavarian!
SPOIT!

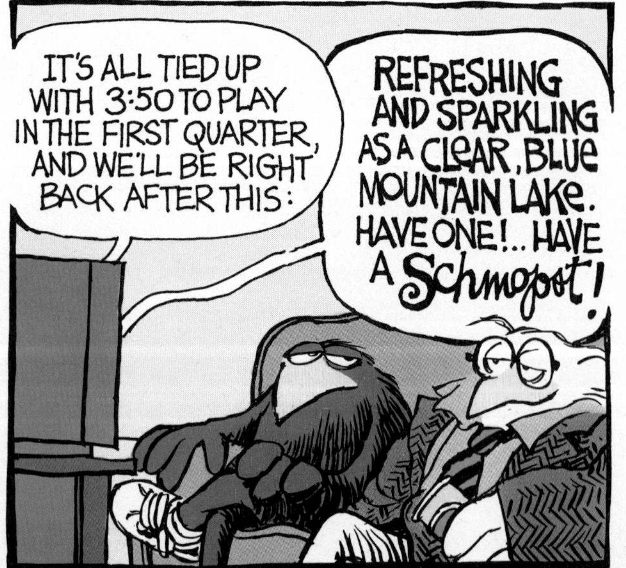

IT'S ALL TIED UP WITH 3:50 TO PLAY IN THE FIRST QUARTER, AND WE'LL BE RIGHT BACK AFTER THIS:
REFRESHING AND SPARKLING AS A CLEAR, BLUE MOUNTAIN LAKE. HAVE ONE!... HAVE A Schmopot!

SPOIT!

AND WE'LL BEGIN OUR HALF-TIME SHOW RIGHT AFTER THIS MESSAGE:
WHEN IT'S TIME TO GOOF OFF... GRAB FOR A FROSTY CAN OF SUDZ!

SPOIT!

THERE'S TIME OUT ON THE FIELD... AND WE'LL BE BACK IN 60 SECONDS...
DON'T FORGET TO PICK UP AN ICE-COLD SIX PACK

SPOIT
SPOIT
SPOIT
SPOIT
SPOIT
SPOIT
MACNELLY 1/15

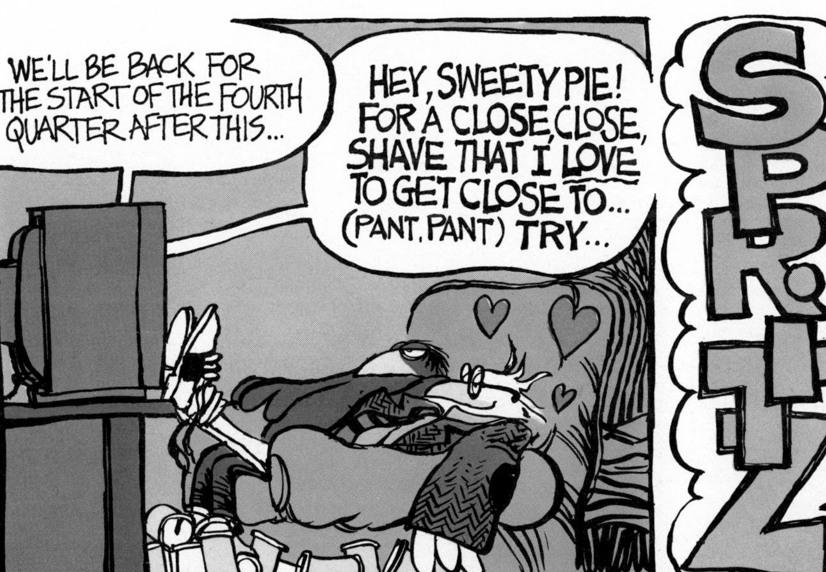
WE'LL BE BACK FOR THE START OF THE FOURTH QUARTER AFTER THIS...
HEY, SWEETY PIE! FOR A CLOSE, CLOSE, SHAVE THAT I LOVE TO GET CLOSE TO... (PANT, PANT) TRY...
SP-R-I-T-Z

I THINK THE BOYS ON MADISON AVENUE HAVE YOU RIGHT WHERE THEY WANT YOU.

THAT REMINDS ME... I BETTER GET GOING ON MY GOURMET FOOD COLUMN...
SANDWICH

The Underground Gourmand
–Prof. Cosmo Fishhawk
No fine meal is complete without wine,

but it's very important to know which wine goes best with which dish.

For example, the ideal companion to red wine is a quality cheese, preferably of a mild variety.

Light red wines are excellent with fowl or veal, while beef and the heavier meats go better with hardier, more robust red wines.

The sweet white wines go particularly well with dessert dishes, such as sweet fruits or puddings.
MACNELLY 1/22

White Burgundy is a delicious companion to Shrimp and lobster.

Chablis, of course, goes superbly with oysters.

AND ROOT BEER IS DYNAMITE WITH TUNAFISH.

HEY...MOVE IT, PERFESSER! IT'S ALMOST TIME FOR THE **NEWS!**

I LOVE WATCHING **WALTER CRONKITE.** HE IS A REAL NEWSMAN'S **NEWSMAN.**

YOU CAN TELL JUST BY LOOKING AT HIM THAT HE DOESN'T REALLY GO FOR ALL THIS SHOW BIZ STUFF.

HE'S A REPORTER JUST LIKE YOU AN' ME.

I BET IF HE HAD HALF A CHANCE HE'D WANT TO BE BACK IN THE NEWSROOM, POUNDING OUT A STORY ON A BEAT-UP OLD TYPEWRITER...
THIS IS THE CBS EVENING NEWS...

WITH ROGER MUDD FILLING IN FOR WALTER CRONKITE, WHO IS OFF SAILING ON HIS YACHT.

MACNELLY 1/29
THINK HE TOOK HIS BEAT-UP OLD TYPEWRITER?

I STILL REMEMBER...

WHEN I WAS A KID THERE WAS THIS BIG **BULLY** DOWN THE BLOCK WHO ALWAYS **BEAT ME UP**.

EVERY SATURDAY LIKE CLOCKWORK THIS GUY WOULD STOMP ON ME ...I'D TRY TO GO OUT BACK AND PLAY...AND **CRUNCH!**... THERE HE'D BE... BASHING ON ME.

IT GOT SO I WAS AFRAID TO GO ANYWHERE ON SATURDAY, 'CAUSE I KNEW AS SOON AS I WENT OUTSIDE, THAT KID WOULD DO A TAP DANCE ON MY FACE.
PROF. COSMO FISHHAWK

FINALLY, MY FATHER DECIDED THAT I NEEDED TO LEARN HOW TO DEFEND MYSELF. SO HE ENROLLED ME IN A **BOXING** CLASS.

SO THEN YOU LEARNED HOW TO FIGHT... AND THE NEXT TIME THAT BIG KID SHOWED UP... YOU WENT INTO THE OLD PEEK-A-BOO DEFENSE AND TAGGED HIM **BWAP!** RIGHT IN THE **LABONZA!..**
WELL... NOT EXACTLY...

FROM THEN ON.... EVERY SATURDAY MORNING I WENT TO THIS DING DONG BOXING ACADEMY AND GOT BEAT UP BY THE INSTRUCTOR.
JEESH.
MACNELLY 2/5

I THINK I'VE GOT OUR FRONT-PAGE HEADLINE...
HEADLINE?! FOR WHAT? THERE'S NOTHING HAPPENING.
TAP TAP TAP

I KNOW, BUT JUST BECAUSE THERE ISN'T ANY EARTH-SHATTERING NEWS DOESN'T MEAN WE DON'T PUT OUT A NEWSPAPER...
TATTLER Tribune

WELL... HERE'S ONE EDITION WE DON'T SUBMIT TO THE PULITZER COMMITTEE.
TATTLER Tribune
CROSSWORD PUZZLE ON PAGE 15
MACNELLY 11/9

THANK YOU FOR NOT SMOKING
MACNELLY 11/10

THANK YOU FOR NOT SMOKING

THANK YOU FOR MINDING YOUR OWN BUSINESS

SHOE... THIS IS THE NO SMOKING SECTION.
WOULD YOU MIND SMOKING THAT RAUNCHY STOGIE ELSEWHERE?

ROZ'S ROOST
SHEESH!
MACNELLY 11/11

THANKS.

ROZ! THERE'S SOMETHING SWIMMING AROUND IN MY COFFEE!
WHAT?!
MACNELLY 11/12

THAT'S IMPOSSIBLE!

IT SURE IS... NOTHING COULD POSSIBLY STAY ALIVE IN THIS STUFF.

RRING!

RRING! RRING!
HELLO? ...HELLO!
11-14
MACNELLY

I HATE PEOPLE WHO HANG UP BEFORE YOU CAN FIND THE PHONE.

CRUMPLE CRUMPLE

HMM...THAT'S WHY THIS PLACE IS SUCH A GARBAGE DUMP...
WHENEVER I HAVE SOMETHING TO THROW OUT...

I CAN'T FIND THE WASTEBASKET.
MACNELLY 11/15

DUE TO EXPLICIT LANGUAGE, THE FOLLOWING PROGRAM IS RECOMMENDED FOR ADULT VIEWING ONLY.

AW, !
MACNELLY 11/16

I'M WORRIED ABOUT YOU, UNCLE COSMO...
HUH?
YOU'VE GOT NO DRIVE, NO ENERGY, NO AMBITION. SOMETIMES I THINK YOU'RE TURNING INTO A BUM!
MACNELLY 11/17.

NOW, SKYLER... YOU CAN STOP WORRYING ABOUT ME.... I'LL NEVER BE A BUM...

THE COMPETITION IS TOO STIFF.

WHAT ARE YOU UP TO NOW, PERFESSER?
I'M JUST REFILING SOME STUFF, SHOE.

REFILING?

LOOKS MORE LIKE A REZONING JOB TO ME.
MACNELLY 11/18
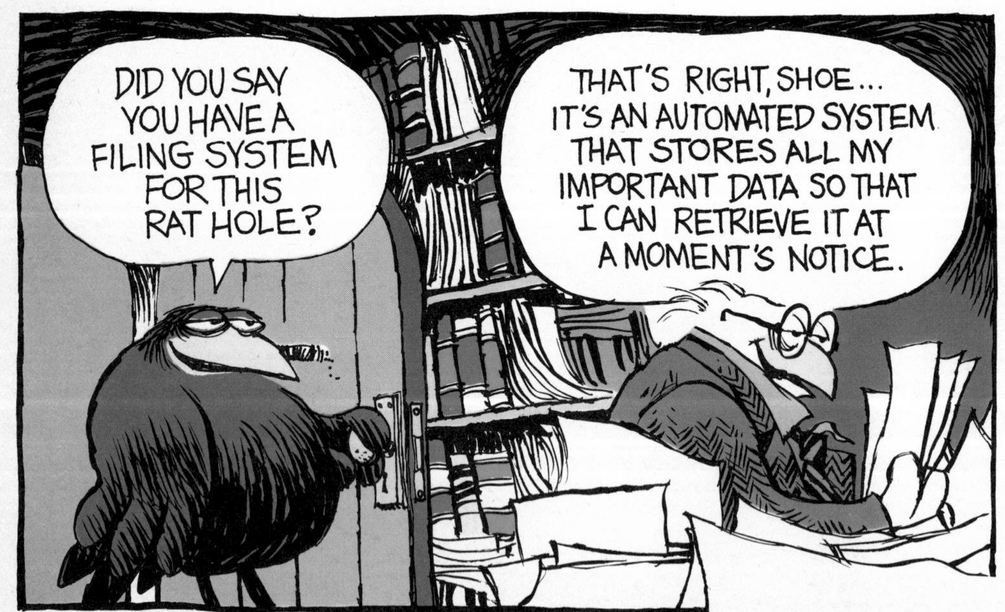
DID YOU SAY YOU HAVE A FILING SYSTEM FOR THIS RAT HOLE?
THAT'S RIGHT, SHOE... IT'S AN AUTOMATED SYSTEM THAT STORES ALL MY IMPORTANT DATA SO THAT I CAN RETRIEVE IT AT A MOMENT'S NOTICE.

YOU MEAN... MICROFILM?
NO...
MACNELLY 11/19

TRASHMASHER
1971 Check Stubs.

BETCHA I CAN TELL YOU WHAT THE SCORE WILL BE BEFORE THE GAME STARTS
YOU'RE ON, PAL.

ZERO TO ZERO

MACNELLY
11/21

PHONE
HEY, OPERATOR! I DIDN'T GET MY DIME BACK!
11/22

I KNOW, SIR... BUT WE'VE GOT A LITTLE OFFICE POOL ON THE RAMS' GAME... AND I THOUGHT YOU MIGHT WANT TO INVEST...
MACNELLY

BOY, THEY DON'T CALL HER OPERATOR FOR NOTHIN'!

HEY! WHAT'RE YOU DOING?
I'M CLEANIN' UP THIS MESS AROUND YOUR DESK.

BUT THAT'S ALL OF MY RESEARCH
11/23
MACNELLY

FOR THE STORY I'M WRITING ON THE LITTER PROBLEM...

11/24
MACNELLY
HERE'S THAT STORY, SHOE... BUT I REALLY HAD TO RUSH IT, AND...
OKAY, OKAY... LET'S HAVE IT, LET'S HAVE IT!

HERE'S PAGE ONE, AND PAGE TWO... BUT...
EDITOR

PAGE THREE MIGHT BE A LITTLE HARD TO READ.
EDITOR

MACNELLY 11/25
LOOK, PERFESSER, I KNOW THESE WEATHER STORIES ARE DULL, BUT THIS THING YOU WROTE REALLY STINKS.
EDITOR

TRY TO JAZZ IT UP A LITTLE, WILL YA?
OH, OKAY...

There is a 30% chance of precipitation, sources close to the Weather Bureau disclosed today.

HEY, SHOE ...HAVE YOU GIVEN MUCH THOUGHT TO HOW WE'RE GOING TO PRINT THIS NEWSPAPER OF OURS?
I MEAN, WE'RE GONNA NEED PAPER AND SOME KIND OF PRINTING PRESS, AREN'T WE?
11/26 MACNELLY

YEAH, YEAH... I GOT IT ALL WORKED OUT.
IN THE INITIAL STAGE, WHILE WE'RE BUILDING UP CIRCULATION...

I FIGURE WE CAN GET BY WITH CARBON PAPER...

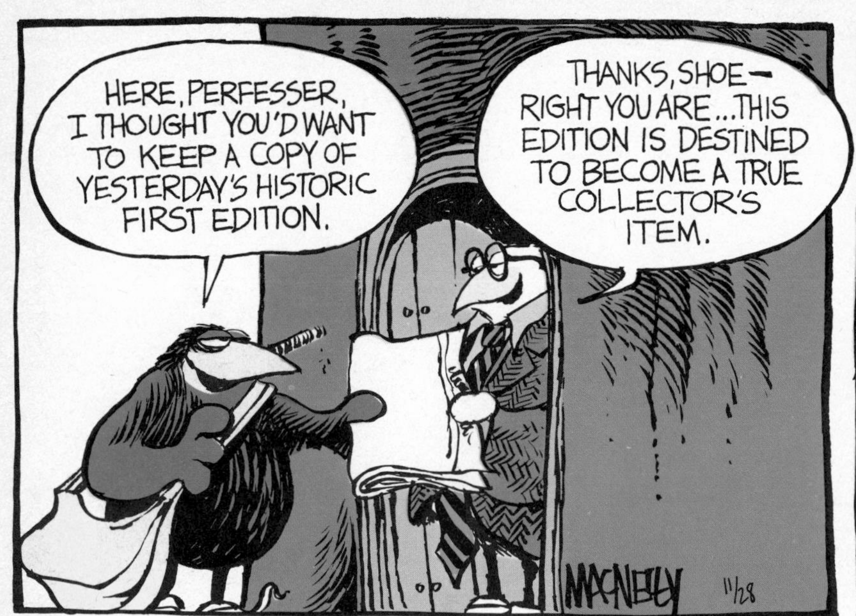
HERE, PERFESSER, I THOUGHT YOU'D WANT TO KEEP A COPY OF YESTERDAY'S HISTORIC FIRST EDITION.
THANKS, SHOE— RIGHT YOU ARE...THIS EDITION IS DESTINED TO BECOME A TRUE COLLECTOR'S ITEM.
MACNELLY
11/28

TRASH COLLECTOR

LOON, GET RID OF THESE EXTRA COPIES OF LAST SUNDAY'S EDITION.
RIGHT, CHIEF!
EDITOR

EXTRA EXTRA!
11/29
MACNELLY

MACNELLY
11/30
TICKA TICKA TACKA TAT

WOW, PERFESSER! YOU SURE CAN TICKLE THAT KEYBOARD!
THANKS... IT'S A TECHNIQUE THAT I DEVELOPED YEARS AGO AT COLLEGE WHEN I HAD TO CRANK OUT A DAILY COLUMN...

I CALL IT HUNT AND PUNT

THRU TRAFFIC
?
MACNELLY 12/1

THRU TRAFFIC
KRASH

SQUEEEKAREE
EEEEEK!
LEARN THE BAGPIPES

SKREEE
I'D LIKE TO REPORT A CHICKEN-STRANGLING IN PROGRESS.
POLICE
MACNELLY 12/2

EEEEEKKASKREE!
SQUAWWWWWK! RRAWK
SQUEEE!
AARGH!... I THINK I JUST VIOLATED THE OLD SCOTTISH LAW OF SURVIVAL:
MACNELLY 12/3

NEVER TUNE YOUR BAGPIPES INDOORS.

AHA! A LETTER ADDRESSED TO "THE LONE PIPER"!

MAYBE IT'S MY FIRST FAN LETTER! ...AND IT APPEARS TO BE IN THE HANDWRITING OF A NICE YOUNG LADY...

...FROM THE NOISE ABATEMENT COMMISSION.
MACNELLY 12/5

OH BOY! OH BOY! THE FIRST SNOW!

JINGLE BELLS! JINGLE BELLS!....
GEE, SHOE... WHAT'S WITH THE PERFESSER?
EDITOR
12/6 MACNELLY

JINGLE ALL THE WAAYYY!!!
I THINK HIS DANDRUFF HAS REACHED THE TERMINAL STAGES.

THE FIRST SNOW... WINTER IS REALLY HERE.

I'D BETTER MAKE SURE I'M WELL INSULATED...

MAGNELLY 12/7
LET'S SEE... I'LL START WITH A COUPLE OF PIECES OF THAT APPLE PIE....

MAGNELLY 12/8

KCHINKA CHINKACHINK
WHAT THE HECK IS THAT?

OH, THAT'S LOON... HE'S TAKING NO CHANCES IN THIS SNOW.
HE BOUGHT A SET OF CHAINS.
CHINKACHINKACHI
CHINKACH
MACNELLY 12/9

HEY, SHOE, I JUST BOUGHT A STEEL-BELTED RADIAL TIRE FOR $53...

YOU THINK THAT'S TOO MUCH?
IT DEPENDS... YOU'LL PROBABLY GET 40,000 MILES OUT OF IT.... SO IT'S NOT A BAD PRICE.

GEE... 40,000 MILES!
MACNELLY 12/10

OKAY, PERFESSER... I'LL TELL YOU WHAT— LET'S TAKE THE TYPEWRITER OVER TO IRVING AND GET IT FIXED.
IRVING? IRVING SEAGULL? BUT HE'S A JUNK DEALER!
EDITO
12/12
MACNELLY

YES, BUT IRVING STANDS BEHIND HIS JUNK...

—HE GAVE ME A 30-DAY WARRANTY ON YOUR MACHINE.

IRV?...THIS TYPEWRITER YOU SOLD ME IS BUSTED.
PROBABLY JUST NEEDS A TUNE-UP... LET'S CHECK IT OUT.
IRVING SEAGULL JUNKSTER
12/13
MACNELLY

IRVING'S
I'M TELLIN' YOU, PERFESSER... THIS GUY'S A MECHANICAL GENIUS.

LOOK, IRV... COULD YOU HURRY IT UP? WE'VE GOT A DEADLINE...

COULD BE A DEAD LINE...
BUT I THINK YOU GOT A DEAD SOLENOID, OR A WORN OUT FIBRILATOR RIM...
MACNELLY 12/14

THE PROBLEM IS WITH THE E, IRV... THE E KEY IS OFF.

AH, YES! RIGHT YOU ARE, SHOE. THE E KEY IS OFF...
IRVING SEAGULL JUNKSTER
MACNELLY 12/15

SOUNDS MORE LIKE F SHARP
SHEER GENIUS.

TELL YOU WHAT... SINCE YOU GUYS BOUGHT THIS MACHINE HERE, I'M GONNA LET YOU TRADE IT IN...

GREAT!
THANKS, IRV!
IRVING SEAGULL JUNKSTER
12/16
MACNELLY

ON THAT 1951 HUDSON HORNET.

HOW CAN WE TRADE THE TYPEWRITER FOR THIS OLD HUDSON... THE CAR CAN'T TYPE, CAN IT?

NO, BUT YOUR TYPEWRITER CAN'T CRUISE AT 85...
SO, I'D CALL IT AN EVEN TRADE
MACNELLY 12/17

TREETOP TATTLER-Tribune
THANKS FOR GETTING ME A NEW TYPEWRITER, SHOE...EVEN THOUGH IT'S ARMY SURPLUS.

HOW DID YOU KNOW THAT?

OH, I COULD JUST TELL.
M-2 TYPEWRITER ONE EACH.
12/19
MACNELLY

RATS! I LOST MY PUCK, UNCLE COZ!

ROZ'S ROOST
COULD WE GET ONE OF YOUR HAMBURGERS TO GO, ROZ?
MACNELLY 12/20

I'VE GOT TWO BIG PROBLEMS TO SOLVE BEFORE I CAN GET READY FOR CHRISTMAS.
12/21
MACNELLY

THE FIRST PROBLEM IS: WHERE AM I GOING TO FIND A TREE?

AND THE SECOND PROBLEM IS, I DON'T KNOW WHERE I PUT LAST YEAR'S DECORATIONS.

...I THINK I JUST SOLVED BOTH.

HEY, SHOE... THERE'S A LITTLE GIRL NAMED VIRGINIA ON THE PHONE...
SHE WANTS TO KNOW IF THERE IS A SANTA CLAUS.

MACNELLY
12/22
HAS SHE TRIED DIRECTORY ASSISTANCE?
EDITOR

COME ON, SHOE! THERE'S A LITTLE GIRL ON THE PHONE WHO WANTS TO KNOW IF THERE IS A SANTA CLAUS... YOU GOTTA SAY SOMETHING!
HMMM...I CAN'T LIE TO HER... BUT I DON'T WANT TO DISILLUSION HER WITH THE TRUTH EITHER...

TELL HER "NO COMMENT."
EDITOR

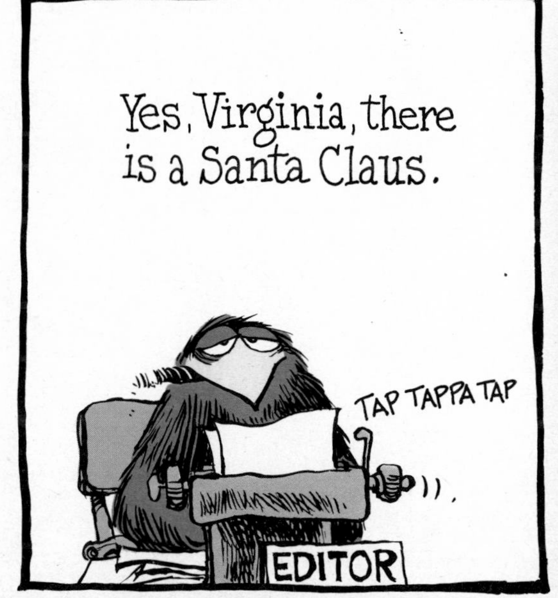
Yes, Virginia, there is a Santa Claus.
TAP TAPPA TAP
EDITOR

He lives in our hearts and in our memories.
TAPPA TAPPA TAP

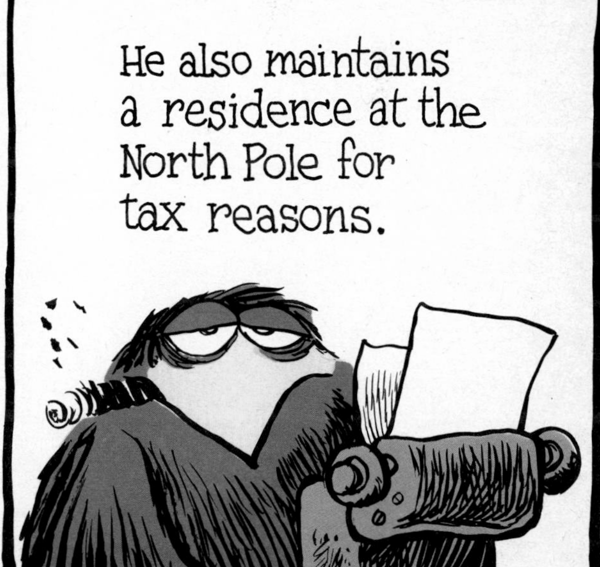
He also maintains a residence at the North Pole for tax reasons.

TIME TO
TRY OUT MY
NEW SLED.

GERONI..

MO.
MACNELLY 12/26

NOTHING
BUT TRASH
TO LOOK AT
TONIGHT!
TV

SAME
TO YOU,
FELLA!
12/27
MACNELLY

PART
C.

TV

MACNELLY 12/28
TV

BEFORE TAKEOFF, MAKE SURE ALL YOUR INSTRUMENTS ARE WORKING PROPERLY
Learning to FLY

LOON
SKREE!
I'M AFRAID TO ASK.
12/29
MACNELLY

HEY, THEY'RE HAVING A SALE AT INSEAM'S
WHY DON'T YOU GET A NEW JACKET, PERFESSER?
INSEAM'S FINE Menswear
SALE

NAH...THEY NEVER HAVE ANYTHING IN A 42 D.
42 D?...
MACNELLY 12/30

42 DUMPY.

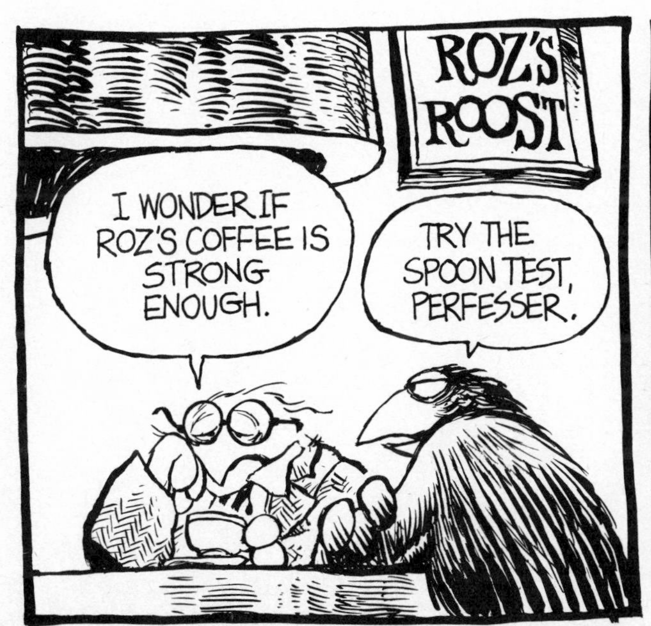
ROZ'S ROOST
I WONDER IF ROZ'S COFFEE IS STRONG ENOUGH.
TRY THE SPOON TEST, PERFESSER.

DIP YOUR SPOON IN THE COFFEE AND IF YOU CAN'T SEE THE END OF IT...

IT'S JUST ABOUT RIGHT.
MACNELLY 12/31

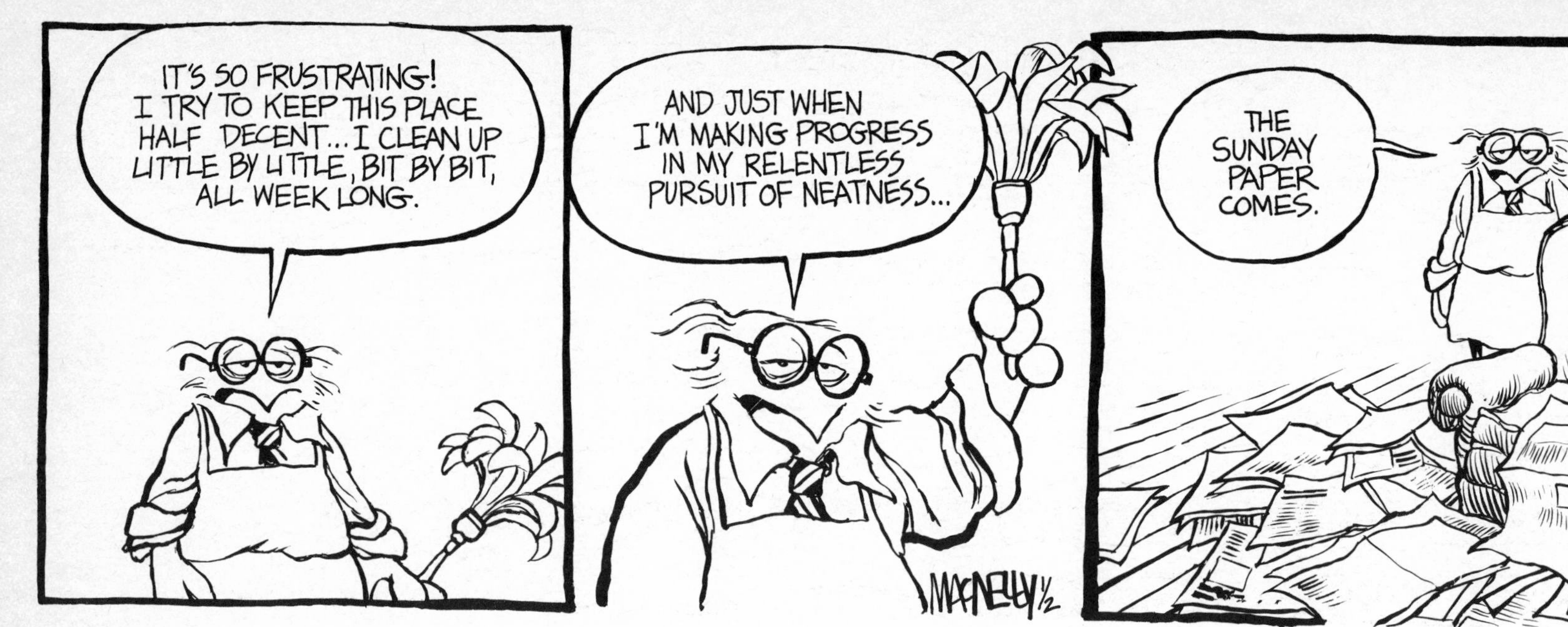
IT'S SO FRUSTRATING! I TRY TO KEEP THIS PLACE HALF DECENT... I CLEAN UP LITTLE BY LITTLE, BIT BY BIT, ALL WEEK LONG.
AND JUST WHEN I'M MAKING PROGRESS IN MY RELENTLESS PURSUIT OF NEATNESS...
MACNELLY 1/2
THE SUNDAY PAPER COMES.

THERE'S NOTHING YUMMIER THAN A MIDNIGHT SNACK!

SOME THINGS TASTE MUCH BETTER IN THE DARK...

I COULD NEVER EAT A COLD BAKED BEAN SANDWICH IF I HAD TO LOOK AT IT, TOO.
MACNELLY 1/3

My boyfriend, Howard, who is a disc jockey, and I are going to visit my mother who is doing 10 years at the Pen for grand theft-auto. She needs an operation, but she's been broke ever since Daddy ran off with the Avon lady back in '67. My brother won't help her – He's a wino and steals from his own kids to keep himself in Muscatel. My question is this:

An Editorial
by P. Martin Shoemaker, Editor
This newspaper has always been in favor of clean air. We supported a ban on leaf-burning.

We went along with air quality standards for industry. We supported air-pollution controls for automobiles....

We think, however, that catalytic converters for cigars is pushing it.
MACNELLY 1/6

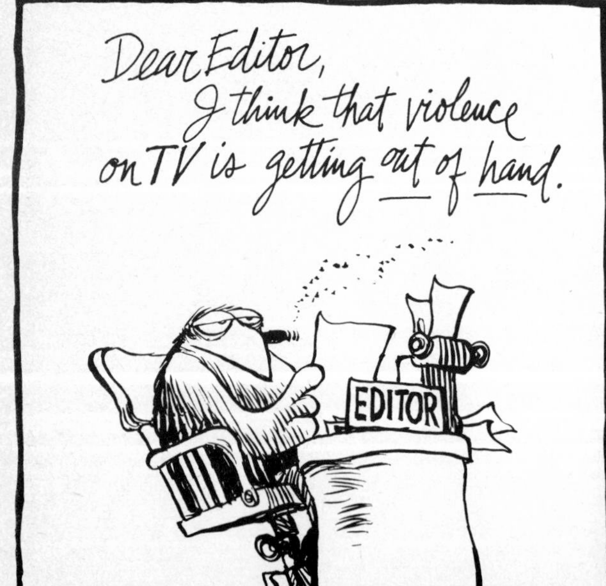
Dear Editor,
I think that violence on TV is getting out of hand.
EDITOR

Parents should monitor the programs their children watch, and if a show is too violent – don't let them watch it!
MACNELLY 1/7

I have told my kid if he watches KOJAK one more time, I'll break his thumbs.

NO, SHOE... NOT ANOTHER KICK-A-CAT EDITORIAL!

IT'S NOT JUST CATS I'M AFTER, PERFESSER. IT'S CAT-LOVERS.

THEY'RE THE ONES RESPONSIBLE FOR THE SHOCKING EXPLOSION IN THE CAT POPULATION. ...THEY'RE INTERFERING WITH THE BALANCE OF NATURE, ACTUALLY... ANYWAY, IT'S TIME WE HAD A RESPONSIBLE **CAT POLICY** IN THIS COUNTRY...

AND THE ONLY WAY WE CAN DO IT IS TO KICK THE **CAT-LOVERS** RIGHT WHERE IT HURTS MOST:

IN THEIR **CATS**

MACNELLY 1/9

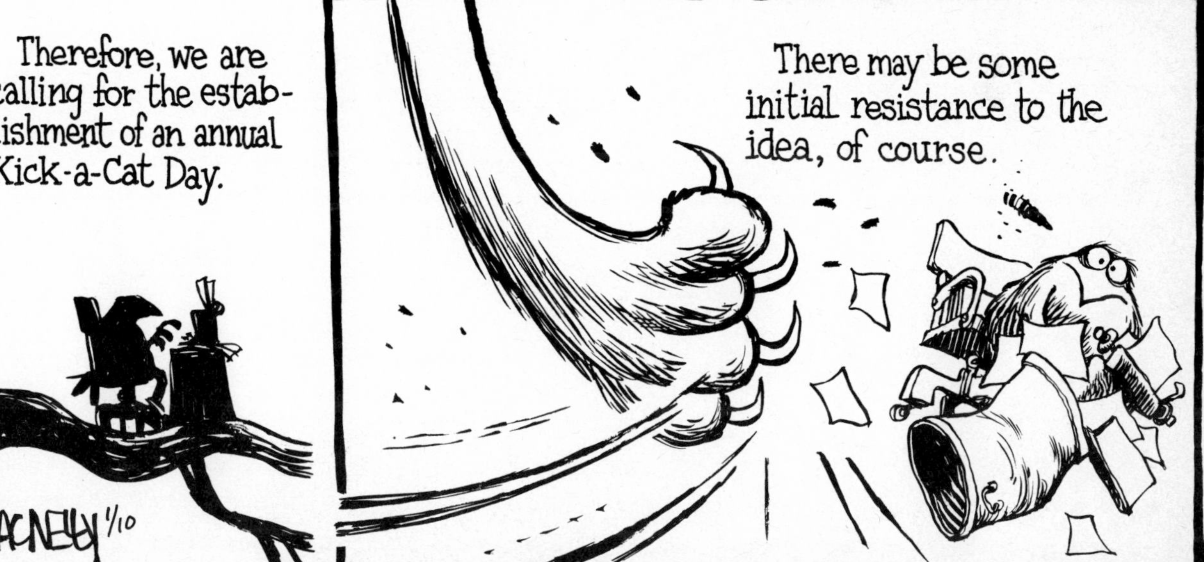

We've decided to hold off for a while on our controversial Kick-a-Cat Day campaign.

There was some question about the usefulness of such a "Day," and many objections were raised by a small, but vocal group of cat-lovers.

Also, the Cat Lobby is more powerful than we thought.

HEY, SHOE... HERE'S A REAL INTERESTING THEORY.

THIS GUY CLAIMS THAT IF YOU TAKE AN INFINITE NUMBER OF MONKEYS AND AN INFINITE NUMBER OF TYPEWRITERS, THEY WOULD EVENTUALLY WRITE ALL THE GREAT WORKS.
IS THAT RIGHT?... HMM...
MACNELLY 1/12
THAT MEANS A COUPLE OF GOOD CHIMPS COULD CRANK OUT ONE OF YOUR COLUMNS EVERY 15 MINUTES.

I'M STARVING, PERFESSER... CAN I RAID YOUR ICEBOX?
SURE... HELP YOURSELF.

HEY, WHAT'S THIS GREEN STUFF?
OH, THAT'S EITHER FRESH SALAD...

OR VERY OLD BACON.
1/13
MACNELLY

GROCERY
HOW DO YOU PICK OUT A GOOD MELON, PERFESSER?

SIMPLE...YOU GRASP THE MELON THUSLY... AND THWACK IT LIKE THIS...

AND IF NOTHING SCAMPERS OUT, IT'S OKAY.
1/14
MACNELLY

I'VE COME UP WITH A RESTAURANT RATING SYSTEM FOR MY FOOD COLUMN.
FROM POOR, (ONE FORK) TO EXCELLENT, (FIVE FORKS...)
OH YEAH?... HOW DO YOU RATE ROZ'S PLACE?
ROZ'S GETS A SHOVEL.
TRASH
MACNELLY 1/16

GOTTA WRITE A WRAP-UP ON LAST NIGHT'S CITY COUNCIL MEETING.
SOMETHING SHORT AND SWEET...
THAT CAPTURES... ER... THE WHOLE... FLAVOR... OF... UH..
Z
TAP
MACNELLY 1/17

HEY, THIS STORY IS TERRIFIC, PERFESSER... GREAT STUFF!
EDITOR

THIS IS THE WAY YOU SHOULD WRITE ALL THE TIME!
THANKS, SHOE... BUT I DIDN'T, ER, WRITE THAT...
EDITOR

OF COURSE YOU DIDN'T WRITE IT, DIMWIT! I DID! I'M JUST SAYING THIS IS THE WAY YOU SHOULD WRITE!!....
MACNELLY 1/18

MACNELLY 1/19
AH, IRVING! THANKS FOR COMING. THE FURNACE IS ON THE BLINK AGAIN.

IT'S RIGHT THROUGH THERE, IN THE UTILITY ROOM.
CHECK.

WHERE IN THE UTILITY ROOM?...

DID YOU FIND THE PROBLEM WITH THE FURNACE, IRV?...
I'M HALFWAY THERE...
MACNELLY 1/20

I FOUND THE FURNACE.

AS LONG AS YOU'RE HERE, IRV, COULD YOU CHECK OUT MY TYPEWRITER?
SURE.

I TRIED TO FIX IT MYSELF... I EVEN READ THE OWNER'S MANUAL...

UH, PERFESSER, THIS HERE'S THE OWNER'S MANUAL TO A '58 BUICK.
WELL... THAT EXPLAINS WHY I COULDN'T FIND THE EMERGENCY BRAKE.
MACNELLY

HELLO?... NO, SORRY... SHOE'S NOT HERE. HE'S OUT ON ASSIGNMENT.

MACNELLY 1/23
ASSIGNMENT
TREETOPS, VA.

THIS HAS GONE TOO FAR! NO MORE EATIN' AT YER DESK!!

SIGH I GUESS THAT WILL BE ALL, BUMPKINS... PUT THE CHOCOLATE MOUSSE IN A DOGGY BAG, IF YOU WOULD...
MACNELLY 1/24

Sandwiches

MACNELLY 1/25
WHAT'S THE SOUP DU JOUR?

I BELIEVE I'LL HAVE THE TASTELESS HAM AND CHEESE SANDWICH
Sandwich

WITH THE CLAMMY SLAB OF CHEESE AND A RUBBERY, GRAY SLIVER OF HAM ON SQUISHY WHITE BREAD... HOLD THE MAYO.

MACNELLY 1/26
THIS STUFF ISN'T TOO BAD, REALLY... IF YOU DON'T GET YOUR HOPES UP TOO HIGH.

HEY... HERE'S A GUY WHO GOT IN THE GUINNESS BOOK OF WORLD RECORDS TWICE FOR THE SAME STUNT.

"WORLD'S LONGEST MOTORCYCLE JUMP OVER A SHARK-INFESTED SWIMMING POOL" AND....

MACNELLY 1/27
DON'T TELL ME... "WORLD'S LOWEST IQ."

I'M NOT AS BIG A SLOB AS YOU THINK!

IN FACT, I HAVE A FILE FOR EVERYTHING IN MY OFFICE...

MACNELLY 1/28
EVERY-THING
MISC.

OH RATS!...
THAT LIBRARY BOOK
I HAVE TO RETURN...

IT'S BURIED
UNDER A MONTH
OF STUFF...

LOOKS LIKE
WE'LL HAVE TO
BLAST.
COSMO
MACNELLY 1/30

THERE!
IT TOOK A
WHILE, BUT...

I FINALLY
GOT IT ALL
TOGETHER.
MACNELLY 1/31

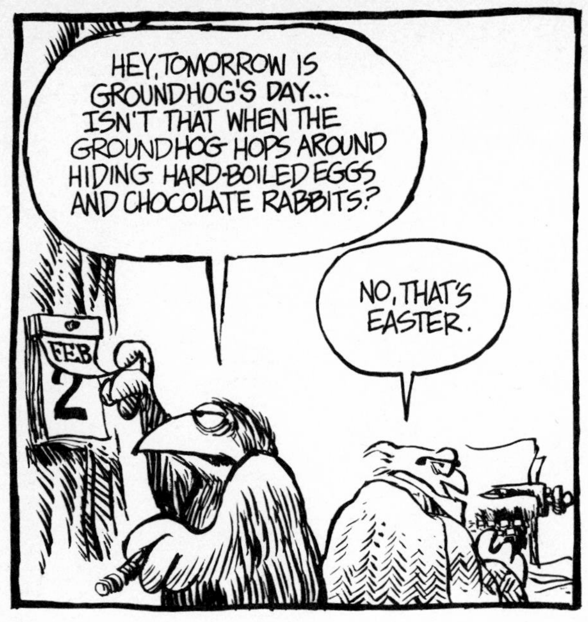
HEY, TOMORROW IS GROUNDHOG'S DAY... ISN'T THAT WHEN THE GROUNDHOG HOPS AROUND HIDING HARD-BOILED EGGS AND CHOCOLATE RABBITS?
NO, THAT'S EASTER.
FEB 2

OH YEAH... THE GROUNDHOG IS THE FAT GUY WHO SLIDES DOWN CHIMNEYS AND LEAVES GOODIES FOR ALL THE KIDDIES.
NO... THAT'S SANTA CLAUS... THE GROUNDHOG COMES OUT OF HIS HOLE ON FEBRUARY 2, AND IF HE SEES HIS SHADOW, HE GOES BACK TO SLEEP AND WE GET SIX MORE WEEKS OF WINTER.

THAT'S ALL?.. NO CANDY...? NO PRESENTS? NO FEASTING? ...NO CARDS?

WAKE UP, DUMMY! YOU NEED AN AGENT!
GROUND-HOG
MACNELLY 2/1

G'MORNING, GROUNDHOG!... I'M YOUR NEW AGENT.
ZZZZ... GARUMPF...

PUT 'ER THERE, PARTNER!
?

ZIP

WHAT DID I DO?...
YOU PUT SPRINGTIME ON "HOLD"... I THINK.
GROU
HO
MACNELLY 2/2

AH...**HOCKEY!** WHAT A TERRIFIC SPORT!...

FAST-PACED AND ACTION-PACKED...AND GLIDING AROUND OUT HERE IS TREMENDOUS EXERCISE TOO...

OF COURSE, IT IS A LITTLE HARD ON THE ANKLES.
MACNELLY 2/3

AH!...BEHOLD THE INTREPID WINTER SPORTSMAN!

—ALONE, BUT UNDAUNTED AMONGST THE HARSH ELEMENTS, CHALLENGING MOTHER NATURE AND THE GREAT OUTDOORS IN THE POETIC PURSUIT OF THE JOY OF SPORT!

MACNELLY 2/4
WHAT'S SO POETIC ABOUT COOLING DOWN A SIX-PACK?

PERFESSER... I'VE DECIDED TO PROMOTE YOU TO THE NEWLY CREATED POST OF ADVENTURE EDITOR

ADVENTURE EDITOR?

MACNELLY 2/6.

YOU'LL BE FREE TO TRAVEL ALL AROUND AND DO FAR-OUT, EXOTIC STORIES ON ANYTHING YOU WANT... YOUR ONLY RESTRICTION IS THE BUDGET...

GOSH...I COULD GO DIVING WITH CAPT. COUSTEAU...CLIMB THE HIMALAYAS....SAIL THE PACIFIC...RIDE A DUGOUT CANOE UP THE AMAZON....

WHICH IS $5.61.

OR TAKE THE GREYHOUND TO SHORT PUMP.

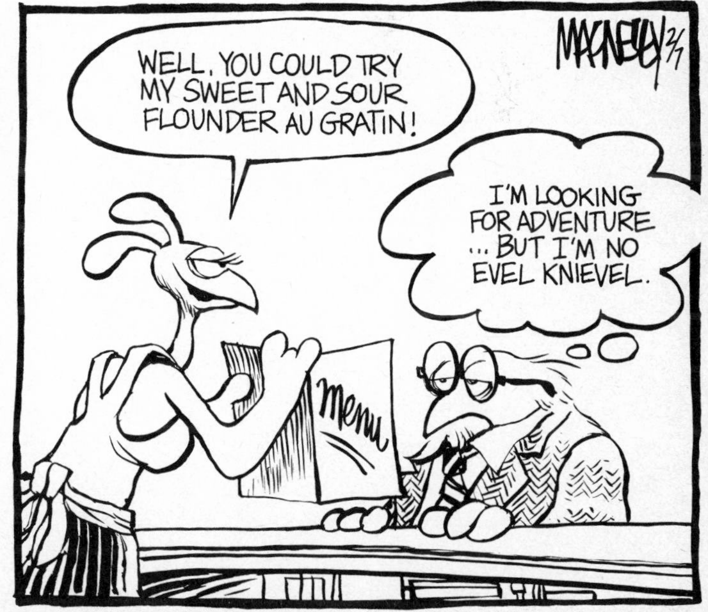

COME ON NOW, PERFESSER! THERE ARE ALL KINDS OF EXCITING THINGS YOU COULD DO FOR $5.61...

JUST USE YOUR IMAGINATION... CLOSE YOUR EYES AND THINK OF THE WILDEST POSSIBLE ADVENTURE YOU'VE EVER DREAMED OF!
ROZ'S ROOST

AH, YES!

MACNELLY 2/8
I'LL BUY A SIX-PACK AND WATCH "AN EVENING WITH THE BOSTON POPS!"

BACK FROM A THRILLING ADVENTURE, PERFESSER?
EDITOR

WELL, I HAD LUNCH AT ROZ'S...

MACNELLY 2/9
IT WAS AS CLOSE AS I COULD COME TO DEATH-DEFYING ADVENTURE ON MY LIMITED BUDGET.

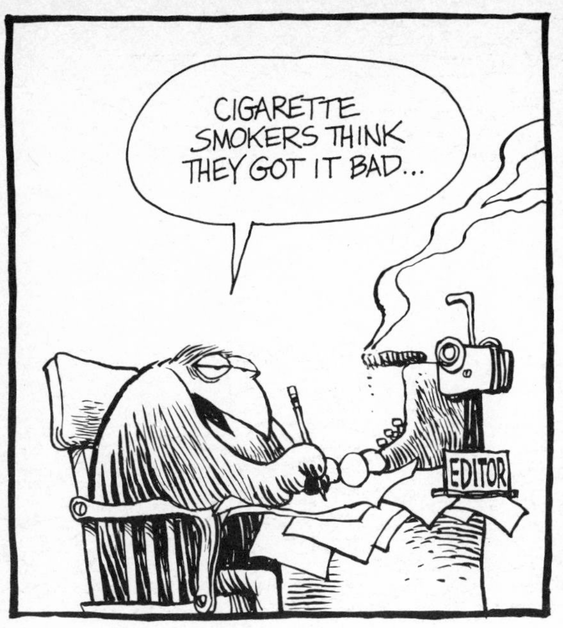
CIGARETTE SMOKERS THINK THEY GOT IT BAD...
EDITOR

ALL THEY HAVE TO WORRY ABOUT IS A LITTLE WARNING FROM THE SURGEON GENERAL

MACNELLY 2/10
WHILE WE CIGAR SMOKERS HAVE TO FILE QUARTERLY REPORTS WITH THE STATE AIR POLLUTION CONTROL BOARD.

THERE'S NOTHING IN THE WORLD QUITE LIKE FIRING UP THE FIRST CIGAR OF THE DAY.

AHH!.... THE AROMA! IT'S LIKE ... ER... LET'S SEE, IT'S HARD TO FIND WORDS TO DESCRIBE IT... —IT'S LIKE...

MACNELLY 2/11
LOW TIDE IN PERTH AMBOY, NEW JERSEY.
EDIT

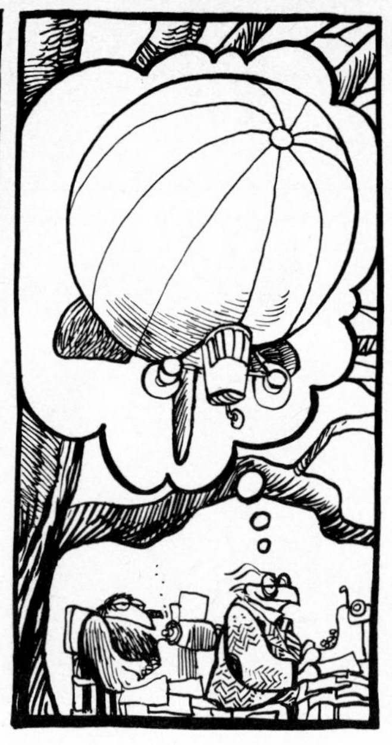

MACNELLY 2/13
AWRIGHT! CUT OUT THE DAYDREAMIN' AN' GET THE HECK BACK TO WORK!

YUK! ANOTHER VALENTINE'S DAY... HOW THOROUGHLY DEPRESSING.

EVERY YEAR IT'S THE SAME OLD THING...
Prof. Cosmo Fishhawk
MACNELLY 2/14

I GET A CARD WITH A TORRID, PASSIONATE LITTLE MESSAGE, SIGNED MYSTERIOUSLY: "GUESS WHO!"

IN MOM'S HANDWRITING.

SHOE, YOU'RE JUST NOT GIVING MY BLIMP PROJECT A FAIR SHOT...

THINK OF ALL THE PRACTICAL APPLICATIONS OF THE NOBLE AIRSHIP TO MODERN LIFE, TRANSPORTATION, COMMUNICATION, INDUSTRY...

THINK OF WHAT THE BLIMP COULD DO TO IMPROVE THE LOT OF MANKIND!
MAYBE YOU'RE RIGHT, PERFESSER...
MACNELLY 2/15

IF YOU CALL GETTING GREAT OVERHEAD TV SHOTS AT THE AVOCADO BOWL IMPROVING THE LOT OF MANKIND.

THINK OF THE ADVERTISING POSSIBILITIES OF A BLIMP, SHOE...
TREETOPS TATTLER-TRIB. BLIMP PLANS

WE COULD RENT OUT THE SPACE ON THE SIDE TO ADVERTISERS!
CAN YOU IMAGINE, SHOE, A MASSIVE, FLYING BILLBOARD WITH GREAT, HUGE LETTERS ON THE SIDE SAYING...
MACNELLY 2/16

"FOR SALE – '63 CHEVY 8 CYL. AUTO. TRANS, AIR, CLEAN. MAKE OFFER."

YOU CALL THIS A STORY? WHAT ARE YOU, SOME KINDA BLITHERING TURKEY?!

EDITOR

"STICKS AND STONES MAY BREAK MY BONES, BUT WORDS CAN NEVER...

MACNELLY 2/17

ZING

EDITOR

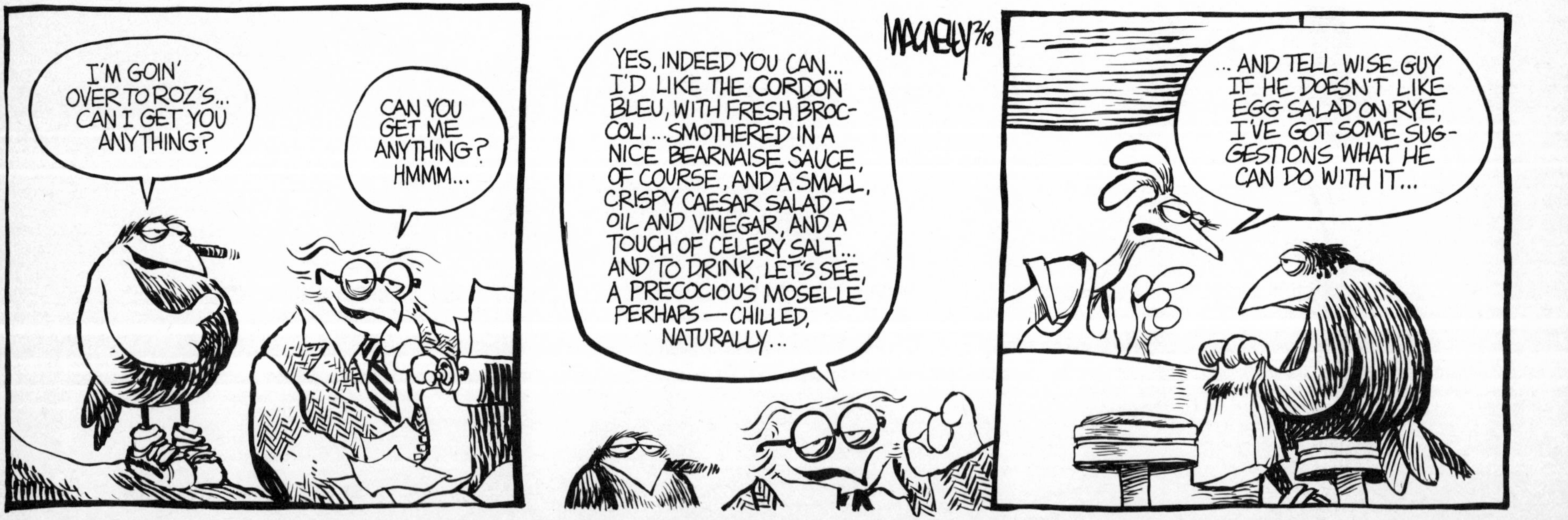

I'M GOIN' OVER TO ROZ'S... CAN I GET YOU ANYTHING?

CAN YOU GET ME ANYTHING? HMMM...

YES, INDEED YOU CAN... I'D LIKE THE CORDON BLEU, WITH FRESH BROCCOLI... SMOTHERED IN A NICE BEARNAISE SAUCE, OF COURSE, AND A SMALL, CRISPY CAESAR SALAD—OIL AND VINEGAR, AND A TOUCH OF CELERY SALT... AND TO DRINK, LET'S SEE, A PRECOCIOUS MOSELLE PERHAPS—CHILLED, NATURALLY...

MACNELLY 2/18

...AND TELL WISE GUY IF HE DOESN'T LIKE EGG SALAD ON RYE, I'VE GOT SOME SUGGESTIONS WHAT HE CAN DO WITH IT...

LET ME SEE THE FINANCIAL SECTION...
EDITOR

BUT THAT'S THE SPORTS PAGE.

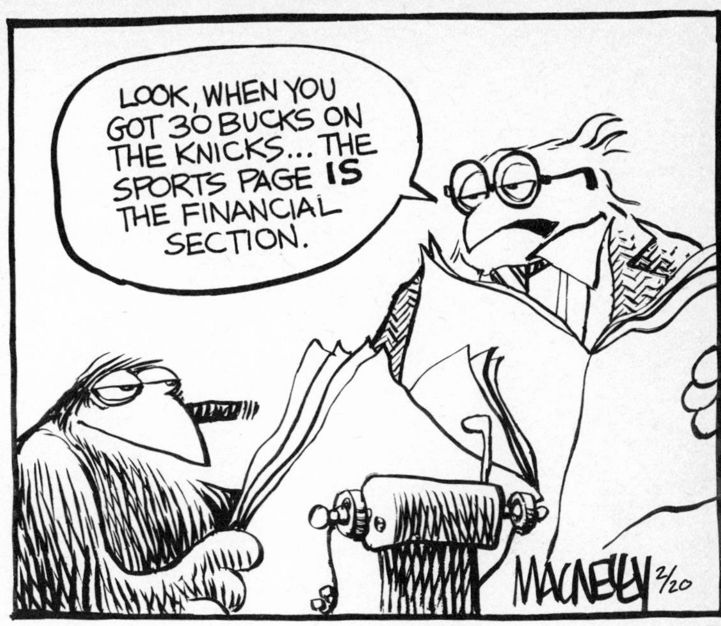
LOOK, WHEN YOU GOT 30 BUCKS ON THE KNICKS... THE SPORTS PAGE **IS** THE FINANCIAL SECTION.
MACNELLY 2/20

RRRING
Prof. COSMO FISHHAWK

I WONDER WHY WE BIRDS DON'T HIBERNATE

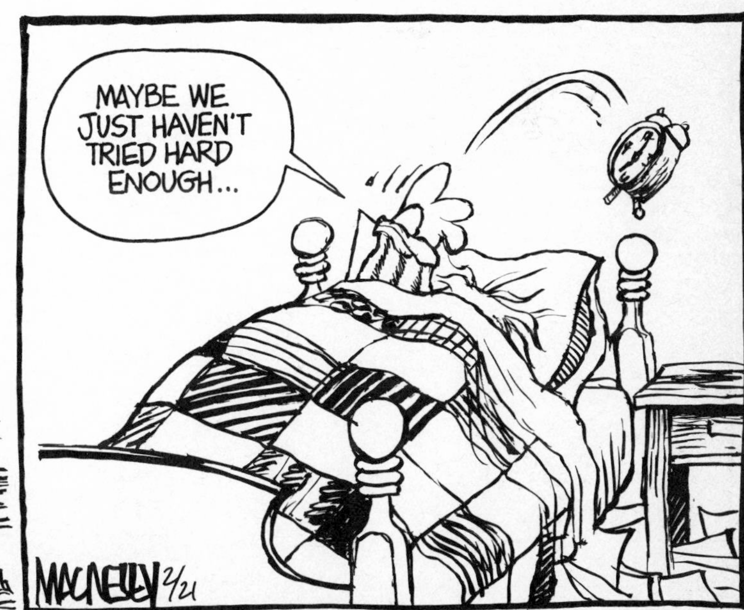
MAYBE WE JUST HAVEN'T TRIED HARD ENOUGH...
MACNELLY 2/21

Memo:
To: All personnel
From: the Editor
OUT
EDITOR
IN

Effective immediately, in order to cut down on the disgraceful waste, this office will begin RECYCLING paper whenever possible.

MACNELLY 2/22
OUT
EDITOR
IN

HEY, PERFESSER, DIDN'T YOU READ MY MEMO?
YOUR DECREE ABOUT CLEANING UP MY DESK? YEAH, I SAW IT....

BUT I BET YOU CAN'T FIND IT IN THAT MESS...
I HAPPEN TO KNOW EXACTLY WHERE I PUT IT, SHOE

MACNELLY 2/23
IT'S THE ONLY THING IN MY WASTEBASKET.

I FINISHED THAT STORY YOU WANTED, SHOE.
EDITOR

BUT IT'S A LITTLE LONG, SO YOU MIGHT WANT TO CUT IT A LITTLE.
MACNELLY 2/24

GADZOOKS AND YUKKY!... THAT GARLIC PIZZA I ATE LAST NIGHT REALLY DID IT. MY MOUTH TASTES LIKE SOME-THING CRAWLED IN THERE AND DIED.

THERE'S ONLY ONE REMEDY I KNOW OF...

A LITTLE "HAIR OF THE DOG" FOR BREAKFAST.
MACNELLY 2/25

- HAVE TO DO ANOTHER ONE OF THOSE DUMB MAN-IN-THE-STREET INTERVIEWS.

PARDON ME, SIR...
MACNELLY 2/27

ROZ IS ON THE PHONE... SHE'S GOT A COMPLAINT ABOUT THE WOMEN'S PAGE!
EDITOR

YES, ROZ?...
TRASH

NO, WE WILL NOT CALL IT THE PERSONS' PAGE!

MACNELLY 2/28
RADICAL!
EDITOR

MACNELLY 3/1

EDITOR

HE'S SO OBNOXIOUS WHEN HE DOES HIS MUSIC REVIEWS.

EDITOR

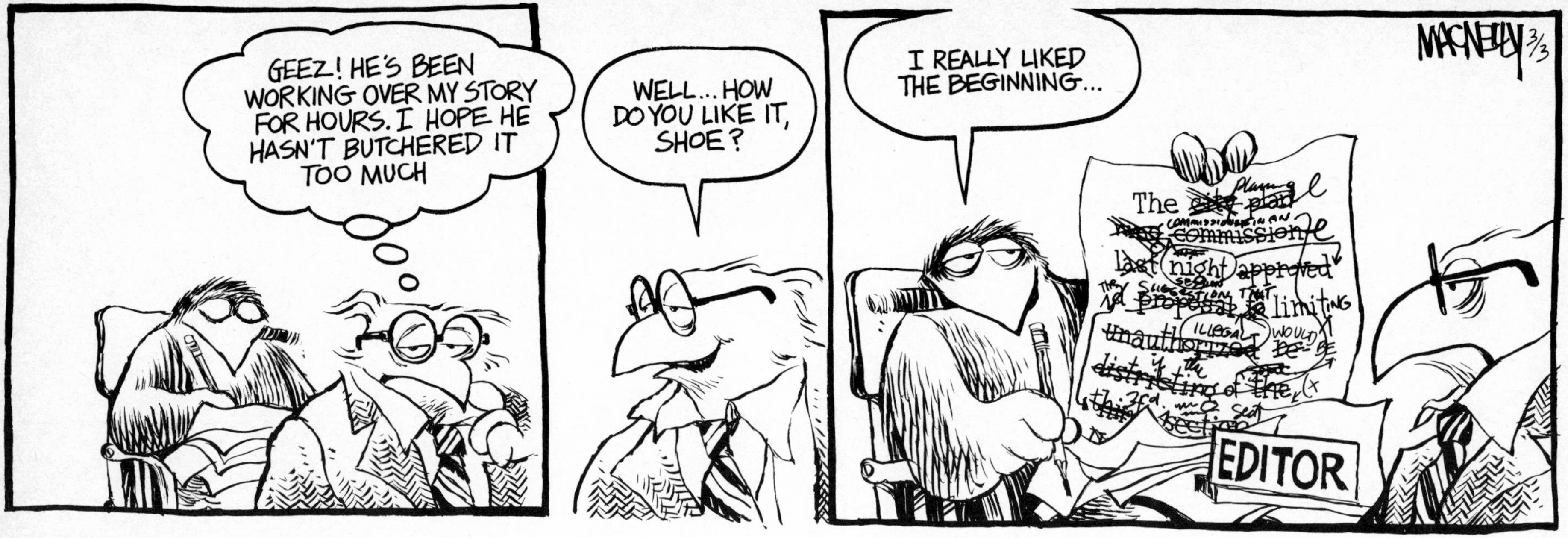

GEEZ! HE'S BEEN WORKING OVER MY STORY FOR HOURS. I HOPE HE HASN'T BUTCHERED IT TOO MUCH

WELL... HOW DO YOU LIKE IT, SHOE?

MACNELLY 3/3

I REALLY LIKED THE BEGINNING...

EDITOR

MACNELLY 3/7

ROOST

I THINK OL' DEADEYE HAS FOUND THE RANGE...